Michael Moore's
Fahrenheit 9/11

CULTUREAMERICA

Karal Ann Marling
Erika Doss
Series Editors

Michael Moore's
Fahrenheit 9/11

How One Film
Divided a Nation

Robert Brent Toplin

University Press
of Kansas

Published by the University Press of Kansas (Lawrence, Kansas 66045), which was organized by the Kansas Board of Regents and is operated and funded by Emporia State University, Fort Hays State University, Kansas State University, Pittsburg State University, the University of Kansas, and Wichita State University

Library of Congress Cataloging-in-Publication Data

Toplin, Robert Brent, 1940-
  Michael Moore's Fahrenheit 9/11 : how one film divided a nation / Robert Brent Toplin.
      p.   cm. — (CultureAmerica)
Includes bibliographical references and index.
ISBN 0-7006-1452-4 (cloth : alk. paper)
  1. Fahrenheit 9/11 (Motion picture) I. Title. II. Title:
Michael Moore's Fahrenheit nine eleven. III. Series:
Culture America.
  PN1997.2.F34T66 2006
  791.43′72—dc22   2006000122

British Library Cataloguing-in-Publication Data is available.

Printed in the United States of America
10 9 8 7 6 5 4 3 2 1

CONTENTS

A photograph section appears following page 82.

Introduction

On March 23, 2003, the provocative and controversial filmmaker Michael Moore walked up to the stage at the Kodak Theatre in Los Angeles to receive an Academy Award for his film *Bowling for Columbine*. Instead of expressing gratitude to producers, agents, and fellow artists, as most award recipients do, Moore shocked the audience. He accused the president of the United States of starting an unnecessary war in Iraq (U.S. bombing had begun just four days earlier). "We like nonfiction and we live in fictitious times," Moore told the hundreds present in the theater and the millions in the United States and abroad watching on television. "We live in a time with fictitious election results that elect fictitious presidents. We live in a time when we have a man sending us to war for fictional reasons." Moore then admonished the president for leading the attack on Iraq. "Shame on you, Mr. Bush," he exclaimed. "Shame on you." In those 45 seconds, Moore summarized the thesis he delivered in the form of a provocative 122-minute movie a little more than a year later.

Some in the audience at the Kodak Theatre applauded, but others drowned out those expressions of approval with loud boos. The award winner was then quickly spirited off the stage while the orchestra struck up a brief musical interlude. A few minutes later, host Steve Martin attempted to break the tension with a joke. "It was so sweet backstage," said the comedian. "You should have seen it. The teamsters are helping Michael Moore into the trunk of his limo."

For several days after that memorable night at the Kodak Theatre, newspapers, radio programs, and politically oriented television shows featured abundant expressions of both support and outrage regarding Michael Moore's comments. Some praised the filmmaker for challenging Hollywood's superficial frivolity and reminding Americans of the terrible destruction that was occurring in Iraq. Moore "may be crazy," wrote Steve Persall in the St. *Petersburg (Florida) Times*. "But it just may be the lunatic we're looking for." Perhaps his controversial antics were necessary,

Persall reasoned, because Moore "might be right."[1] Others criticized the filmmaker for squeezing his political opinions into an event that was supposed to symbolize a celebration of art and entertainment. They claimed that his behavior was rude and inappropriate. An angry editorial in the *Chicago Sun-Times* succinctly communicated the anger felt by many who were appalled not only by Moore's manners but also by his politics. The *Sun-Times* writer noted that while American soldiers were risking their lives on Iraqi battlefields, the "egomaniac" Moore chose to "prance and strut on the stage, spewing rantings that amount to 'a tale told by an idiot, full of sound and fury, signifying nothing.'"[2]

The controversy over Moore's remarks at the Hollywood ceremonies provided a small example of the much larger debate that erupted a year later regarding his provocative documentary film. Like his brief speech at the Kodak Theatre, Moore's *Fahrenheit 9/11* excited both cheers and condemnation. Enthusiasts of the movie hailed Moore's courage in assailing the president and his policies. They claimed that no other creator of films or television programs had so boldly questioned the nation's leadership, particularly President Bush's mistaken reactions to the 9/11 crisis. Critics of the film expanded on the post-Oscar complaints. They called Moore a liar who distorted facts and manipulated evidence for his own malicious purposes. Some compared him to Nazi minister of propaganda Joseph Goebbels and to Hitler's favorite creator of nationalistic documentary movies, Leni Riefenstahl. Conservatives and even some liberals expressed discomfort with Moore's extreme partisanship. They described him as the Left's answer to the Right's Rush Limbaugh and Ann Coulter. In the fashion of those strident polemicists, they said, Moore favored shouts over reasonable discourse.

The stakes in these conflicting viewpoints seemed large at the time, because Michael Moore's film broke attendance records. For the first time in Hollywood's modern history, a documentary film held the top position in audience appeal during its opening weekend. Within a week, *Fahrenheit 9/11* fell behind *Spider-Man 2* in the rankings, but it remained a tremendous attraction for a lengthy period during the summer of 2004. During its first month of distribution, *Fahrenheit 9/11*'s draw surpassed $100 million, an unprecedented financial take for a nonfiction, nonconcert film. That record was even more impressive in view of the limited number of venues that featured the movie. Some theater owners did not schedule the film because they did not expect a documentary to draw well, or they objected to its political perspective and refused to screen it. Where it did show, *Fahrenheit 9/11* often packed the theaters. Moore's film went on to break the opening week attendance record for a documentary film in Great Britain, and it attracted tremendous audience interest when it appeared in Europe, Asia, and the Middle East (some countries there, such as Saudi Arabia and Kuwait, did not permit its screening). Eventually it earned over $200 million worldwide—impressive for a film that cost only $6 million to make.

Fahrenheit 9/11 was more than just a popular documentary film, of course; it was a highly controversial political film that aimed its criticisms directly at the reputation of President George W. Bush and his administration. Like Moore's provocative speech at the Academy Award ceremonies, Fahrenheit 9/11 raised doubts about the president's judgments and questioned the nation's recent international and domestic policics in fundamental ways. It provoked strong reactions. Most people who watched the movie could not judge its messages unemotionally and came away with intensely positive or negative feelings about it. From the first days of Fahrenheit 9/11's appearance in U.S. theaters, Moore's defenders and detractors became locked in a struggle to label the picture a success or a failure, a work of insight or an example of distortion.

Much like the boos that overpowered the applause at the Kodak Theatre in 2003, protests against Moore's film began to overpower expressions of praise for it during the summer of 2004. The main thrust of criticism against Fahrenheit 9/11 came from partisans on the Right. Conservative writers and speakers, Republican politicians, and advocates of President George W. Bush's domestic leadership and foreign policics gave particularly damning assessments. Their efforts to characterize the production as polemical and excessively partisan succeeded to a considerable degree, as did their attempt to cast doubt on the reputation of the filmmaker. Interestingly, many purportedly nonpartisan representatives of the national news media joined them in criticizing Moore and his movie. Of course, millions of viewers greatly appreciated the film and recommended it to others, but a steady stream of negative comments about Fahrenheit 9/11 made an impact. Many newspaper readers, radio listeners, television viewers, and Internet users began to get the impression that Moore's production was problematic, to say the least. They sensed that the controversial motion picture had been discredited in public discussions and should not be praised with enthusiasm in sophisticated company. Some who appreciated Moore's complaints about the Bush administration's policies and the Iraq war were reluctant to give the traditional thumbs-up sign of approval.

This tentativeness was evident when Congressman Charles Rangel, a Democrat from New York City, appeared on CNN's *Crossfire* to speak in defense of the movie. Rangel, who had fought in Korea and received a Purple Heart and Bronze Star, praised *Fahrenheit 9/11* for raising legitimate questions about how the Bush administration had directed U.S. anger over the 9/11 attacks toward a bloody and costly war in Iraq. Rangel pointed to the many American soldiers who had already died in Iraq and asked how many more casualties Americans should tolerate in a war that seemed unnecessary. Cohost Tucker Carlson, representing the conservative position, quickly attempted to redirect the discussion. Carlson objected to some specific words and images in the film, claiming that the movie suggested that "terrible" American soldiers in Iraq were "doing horrible things" and that President George W. Bush "took money from the bin Laden family." By the time Carlson was finished hammering at Rangel, he had created the impression that anyone who supported Moore's "irresponsible" and "outrageous" film was not a patriotic American. At that point, Rangel backed off from the praise he had expressed earlier. When Carlson noted that Rangel seemed willing to throw his "prestige" behind the movie and call it a good film, the congressman lost his nerve and protested. "I never said it was a good movie," he exclaimed. "I never said it was a good movie."

The politically motivated efforts to "diss" *Fahrenheit 9/11* evidently made an impact on film scholars as well, for some of them were quite cautious about praising Michael Moore's work. In a November 2004 conference on political documentaries planned under the auspices of the journal *Film & History*, participants were careful to balance favorable and unfavorable perspectives on Moore's artistry. They expressed appreciation for the director's hard-hitting challenge to the Bush administration's policies but recited some of the familiar questions about Moore's filmmaking strategies that had received considerable attention in the mass media. Toward the end of the session, a few scholars in the audience expressed distaste for Moore's strongly biased approach to interpretation and identified Errol Morris's documentary *Fog of War* as a much better model of sophisticated filmmaking. *Fog of War* was less incendiary and more responsibly presented, they argued. Morris tried to make audiences think about war, they said, while Moore preached on the subject of war.

Fahrenheit 9/11 has become recognized in the eyes of many Americans as an embarrassing example of over-the-top cinematic journalism, and Michael Moore has gained a reputation as an extremist and a propagandist.

Like Congressman Rangel and the film studies professionals, many critics of President Bush's policies have not wished to appear naively supportive of the documentary. The carping against *Fahrenheit 9/11*, expressed by prominent figures in the mainstream media as well as political partisans on the Right, succeeded in making many enthusiasts of Moore's thesis tentative about articulating praise for his film.

This book counters the familiar negative impressions of *Fahrenheit 9/11* with a more broad-based assessment of the movie's (and the moviemaker's) art and politics. The study asks: Did Michael Moore interpret recent American history effectively and with sophistication? Did he violate unwritten but generally acknowledged rules concerning responsible communication through documentary cinema? Were the accusations he made in his film true or false? Did his political cinema have an impact on public opinion?

This evaluation leads to the conclusion that some elements in *Fahrenheit 9/11* are, understandably, subject to debate and criticism. Moore took some risks in constructing his production in order to amuse audiences and design a striking thesis. He could have provided his attackers with a smaller target by omitting some nonessential segments of the movie and removing some particularly contentious statements. At some points in the film, Moore's use of language and imagery seems inclined to arouse heated protests. A more cautious handling of his arguments could have made his critics' job more difficult.

This evaluation also recognizes that some individuals who were sympathetic to *Fahrenheit 9/11*'s political perspective raised thoughtful objections when they complained about the ferocity with which Moore attacked the president and his key advisers. Those "friendly" observers suggest that greater subtlety in the interpretation of recent history could have produced a more successful exercise in political persuasion. They believe that a highly partisan film such as *Fahrenheit 9/11* is likely to draw applause from viewers who are already convinced of the validity of Moore's arguments, but the strategy is not likely to convince undecided voters or Americans in the Republican camp. If Moore had produced a hard-hitting indictment of George W. Bush's leadership but conceded that the motives and actions of the president and his key advisers did not always deserve condemnation, he might have received a warmer reception from the American public. Moore sounded too much like the Left's version of Bill O'Reilly, these friendly critics observe. He pressed his partisan case at every opportunity, while refusing to dignify arguments that might contradict his thesis. The result, argue these sympathetic critics, was a simplistic, one-sided interpretation of events that tended to arouse intense expressions of either approval or contempt from blue- and red-state Americans. Moore's polemical approach limited the movie's impact in the national elections, say these friendly critics.

It is not clear, however, that Moore could have been more successful in achieving his purposes if he had communicated his interpretation in more subtle ways. During the year prior to Fahrenheit 9/11's release, Americans had encountered numerous complaints raised in the media about the Bush administration's handling of the war in Iraq and its "War on Terror." Those commentaries aroused only limited public resistance to the administration's policies. Support for President Bush and his political agenda remained quite strong in public opinion polls reported in the first half of 2004. The president looked like a close contender in the coming elections. Challenging the administration with kid gloves evidently had not produced strong results. Michael Moore preferred to try boxing gloves instead. He could never claim that his technique represented the only appropriate form of political criticism; Fahrenheit 9/11 demonstrated just one way of questioning political leadership—his way.

Michael Moore was not likely to address political questions in the manner of documentary filmmaker Errol Morris, television newscaster Tom Brokaw, or journalist Thomas Friedman, just as those notable commentators could not be expected to adopt Moore's techniques. Moore has established himself as a leading practitioner of just one mode of political expression among many distinct approaches. He became well known for registering complaints about people and policies forcefully and humorously. If he had suddenly shifted strategies and adopted a more subtle approach to cinematic persuasion, he probably would not have reached the huge audiences that typically showed up at his movie screenings. The millions who turned out to watch Fahrenheit 9/11 expected to see the exploits of a funny and audacious filmmaker, not a scholarly cineast who conceded points to people who disagreed with his thesis. If Moore had worked under conditions of repressed partisanship, it is likely that his film would have been much less funny and less entertaining. It is likely, too, that his movie would have been less successful at the box office.

The principal question that needs attention, then, is not whether Michael Moore should have produced a different kind of movie but whether the film he did create was truthful in its treatment of recent events. Angry detractors of Fahrenheit 9/11 say that he employed facts incorrectly, distorted information, deliberately lied about the president, and misrepresented recent U.S. history. My analysis suggests that those familiar indictments of Fahrenheit 9/11 are largely mistaken. In fact, the major disagreements between admirers and detractors of Fahrenheit 9/11 are primarily over the interpretation of facts, not whether the facts themselves are true. Moore's principal evidence is not inherently incorrect, but what one makes of it can excite animated disagreement.

Furthermore, the question is not whether Fahrenheit 9/11 delivered the truth to audiences but whether the movie communicated a truth. Moore's arguments in Fahrenheit 9/11 concerned the United States' war making and the subsequent occupation of Iraq. Moore maintained that the war with Iraq was unnecessary and that the occupation was counterproductive in terms of U.S. interests. He focused on the war's unfortunate consequences for both Iraqis and Americans. Moore also claimed that the Bush administration frequently aroused fear about terrorism for political purposes. These are Moore's "truths." Similar interpretations have been argued persuasively by well-informed observers of U.S. politics. Others, taking dramatically different positions and privileging different evidence, discover other "truths."

For instance, some argue that the Bush administration was correct in initiating hostilities against Iraq and keeping U.S. forces in the country. They point out that the Iraqis participated in sophisticated looting activities at various military sites in their country after the U.S. invasion began, and those looters may have driven off with materials used to make weapons of mass destruction (WMDs). Thus, the absence of WMDs in Iraq did not necessarily negate the need for defensive military action by the United States. Furthermore, supporters of U.S. intervention point out that the postwar American presence in Iraq could provide an important impetus for democratic reforms across the Middle East. By guiding the Iraqi people through their first elections in modern times, say these defenders of the Bush administration's actions, U.S. forces supported a model of democracy that could inspire grassroots movements for democratic reforms in neighboring countries.

These "truths" motivate supporters of the United States' military and administrative actions in Iraq to reject Fahrenheit 9/11's principal thesis. Yet defenders of U.S. actions cannot rely on their preference for a different interpretation of the historical evidence to deny Michael Moore's place as a legitimate participant in the debates over recent U.S. involvement in international affairs. To dismiss Fahrenheit 9/11 as flawed journalism, Moore's

critics needed to identify fundamental shortcomings in his use of information. As this analysis indicates, those critics spoke with greater confidence
than their research merited. They tended to avoid direct confrontation with
Moore's principal thesis, trying, instead, to attack around the periphery of
his arguments. Critics gave particular attention to the smaller issues raised
in the first hour of *Fahrenheit 9/11* and made the evidence presented in that
portion of the film the litmus test for judging the film's merits. Yet even in
their complaints about those peripheral details, the critics could not make
a decisive case against the film. That debate, too, was essentially over how
facts should be considered and interpreted, not whether the facts were fundamentally correct.

The angry indictments leveled by Moore's detractors offered little recognition of the filmmaker's significant achievements in crafting an extraordinarily popular and provocative cinematic essay. *Fahrenheit 9/11*'s contributions
to documentary artistry and public discourse on politics are substantial and
deserve notice. Three of those contributions are salient, and each receives
considerable attention in this book.

First, Moore incorporated a good deal of original material in his interpretation. He provided several unique filmic perspectives that gave his production tremendous emotional force. In this sense, he operated like a skilled
historian who makes a distinctive contribution to public understanding by
developing arguments on the basis of important new "primary" sources.

Second, the filmmaker mixed entertainment and information impressively. This is an extraordinary achievement, because documentary producers often find it difficult to balance the twin goals of pleasing audiences and
stirring them to think. An artist can easily veer too strongly in the direction
of one or the other. Moore's critics often focused on the entertaining aspects of *Fahrenheit 9/11*, claiming that he lampooned George W. Bush and
his leadership team in a ridiculous effort to make viewers laugh. A closer
look at Moore's strategies, however, suggests that he managed to combine
amusement and education with unusual skill.

Finally, Moore delivered "higher truths." *Fahrenheit 9/11* contained numerous facts, quotes, interviews, images, sounds, and other stimuli that
provoked thought, and these diverse elements supported a fundamental
conclusion that was, essentially, true. The movie delivered trenchant arguments (developing, as scholars say, a strong thesis), and it defended those
key points effectively. Many of the basic criticisms Moore leveled at political
leaders' reactions to the tragedy of September 11, 2001, turned out to be cor-

rect. News stories that appeared subsequent to the film's production and distribution confirmed the validity of several major arguments developed in Fahrenheit 9/11. That information gave credence to Moore's reports on prisoner abuse, problems with the Patriot Act, the lack of evidence connecting Saddam Hussein and al Qaeda, the absence of WMDs in Iraq's arsenals, discontent among American soldiers in Iraq, and several other matters.

The major debates about Fahrenheit 9/11 are about politics, not about the mechanics and artistry of filmmaking. Los Angeles Times film critic Kenneth Turan made this observation when discussing reactions to Fahrenheit 9/11 in the mass media.[3] Turan observed that many critics of the film were far more interested in defending the Bush administration than in analyzing the movie's aesthetic elements. Yet they tended to conceal their political agendas, acting as if they were simply asking Moore to respect acknowledged standards of excellence in documentary production. Turan's observation is insightful, for political sentiment figured strongly in public disputes about the cinematic qualities of Fahrenheit 9/11.

Turan could have added that detractors often lambasted Michael Moore for partisanship and insisted that a documentary should present "both sides" of a controversy. Yet many of those who delivered the loudest and most strident criticisms of Moore's approach to filmmaking had not established public records as vigorous champions of fair and balanced treatment of political subjects in the national media. Nor were they outspoken in denouncing heavily opinionated perspectives on controversial issues in film, television, and radio that favored the political Right. Many of the angriest public critics of Fahrenheit 9/11's documentary approach happened to be Republicans, leaders of strongly conservative causes, defenders of U.S. policies in Iraq, or avid supporters of President George W. Bush.

This book builds on Turan's insight. It argues that an analysis of Fahrenheit 9/11's significance needs to move beyond a discussion of the production's aesthetics. A consideration of the artistic techniques Moore employed is useful (and it receives attention here), but our understanding of the movie's significance in recent U.S. history is more fully recognized through an examination of its politics. A look at the way Americans greeted and hooted Fahrenheit 9/11 during the tense weeks and months after its release exposes much about the state of U.S. society at the time.

No single work of speechmaking, writing, filmmaking, or television producing sparked as much debate about the direction of U.S. domestic politics and foreign policy as Fahrenheit 9/11 did. Controversies about the movie provoked Americans to make pointed statements about the policies of President George W. Bush and his administration. The film excited lively exchanges about the meaning of September 11 and the appropriateness of the U.S. invasion and occupation of Iraq. It aroused discussions about the long domestic reach of the Patriot Act. The movie stirred many Americans to offer strong opinions about emotion-laden subjects such as the role of the military, the power of the mass media, the nature of conservatism, the danger of censorship, and the meaning of democracy. Debates about *Fahrenheit 9/11* led, also, to fascinating exchanges regarding the ability of committed filmmakers to influence public opinion. For a brief time, there were animated discussions in the national media about whether Moore's film could help John Kerry win the election or whether its partisan approach might backfire and serve the interests of President Bush and Republican candidates in races for the House and Senate.

At the center of these debates, of course, was Michael Moore. Throughout the disputes, he stayed in the public spotlight. Moore remained as noisy and combative during the period of public exchanges about *Fahrenheit 9/11* as he had been at the Academy Award ceremonies in 2003. He appeared at numerous public events and gave many radio and television interviews, flailing away at the Bush administration and defending his film. In the final months of the 2004 election campaign, Moore appeared on college campuses and in public auditoriums in an effort to get Americans to register, vote, and retire George W. Bush from the White House. He called this campaign, which was aimed at young citizens who tended to sit out elections, the Slacker Uprising Tour.

The subject of this study once claimed that there were two Michael Moores: "There's the one that the right-wing lunatics have created," said the filmmaker. "The fictional Michael Moore. The one they just make stuff up about. And then there's me." Who is that individual? Where did he get his ideas, and what are his politics? How does he feel about liberals, Democrats, conservatives, and Republicans? Is he an "anti-American" radical, as some of his detractors claim? Do his films tend to inform or deceive the public? Should his movies be called "documentaries," or are they really examples of "propaganda"?

Chapter 1 examines Moore's personal background, the development of his ideas, and the evolution of his filmmaking. It traces Moore's experiences as a member of a working-class family employed in Michigan's auto

industries and reviews his rather erratic endeavors prior to his success with
Roger & Me (1989). Although that production launched his filmmaking career, there were setbacks and disappointments before he gained new fame
as the author of popular books and the creator of the award-winning film
Bowling for Columbine (2002).

Should Moore's hard-hitting documentary style be identified as propaganda? Kevin Rafferty, a principal creator of the opinionated film *Atomic Café*
and a mentor to Moore, said, "There are two kinds of propaganda: propaganda when you know you're lying and propaganda when you think you're
telling the truth."[4] If *Fahrenheit 9/11* is propaganda, which type is it?

Chapter 2 dissects Moore's controversial movie, noting techniques the
filmmaker employed to establish his political case. It identifies not only the
film's primary messages but also important subsidiary arguments. For instance, the U.S. mass media are a principal target of Moore's film, along
with the Bush administration. He suggests repeatedly that news reporters
and news interpreters failed to alert the American public about the nation's
mistaken policy in the months leading up to the war in Iraq. Especially in
the early sections of the film, Moore appears to uncover suspicious behavior just about every time the Bush administration acts. He suggests the
possibility of a conspiracy regarding the 2000 presidential election, Bush
family ties with the Saudi royal family and the Carlyle Group, and businessmen's plans to construct an oil pipeline in Afghanistan. The flights out of
the United States arranged for Saudi nationals shortly after September 11,
2001, also draw his attention.

Moore built his arguments on a foundation of diverse "primary sources."
He included many distinctive types of film footage in *Fahrenheit 9/11* that
had not received much screening on the network news. Chapter 2 examines how Moore obtained these controversial images and interviews and
how he chose to employ them. My analysis probes the production history
of *Fahrenheit 9/11* to throw light on the director's investigatory techniques. It
also examines the controversies aroused by Moore's employment of these
"primary" materials.

No study of the "anatomy" of *Fahrenheit 9/11* would be complete without
a consideration of Moore's distinctive style. Most notably, he mixes humor
with serious material, a strategy that arouses both praise and loud complaints. The artist defends this approach by claiming that it helps him reach
a wide audience. He attributes his unusual success as a documentary filmmaker to one thing: "I actually put the entertainment and the art before the

politics." It is difficult for someone on the professional Left to put anything ahead of politics, argues Moore, "and that's why they lose out." In chapter 2 I examine these disputes about Moore's artistic style, considering not only the movie's intrinsic characteristics but also its relationship to other forms of entertainment. Moore's penchant for humorous interludes can be better understood in the context of recent trends in news and entertainment programming on television.

Chapter 3 draws its title ("A Sinister Exercise") from the writing of Christopher Hitchens, one of the many pundits who blasted Moore for failing to be truthful. Hitchens, in an oft-quoted indictment, criticized Fahrenheit 9/11 for "moral frivolity, crudely disguised as an exercise in seriousness."[5] This chapter looks closely at the critics' arguments about Fahrenheit 9/11's treatment of historical evidence. Political commentators on radio and television talk shows and many of the nation's leading op-ed columnists weighed in on this issue during the weeks after the film's release. The detractors argued that Moore brought a highly partisan approach to his subject, privileging information that supported his opinions and failing to give screen time to facts that undermined his case. Critics also disparaged the information Moore presented against the policies of George W. Bush. They said that the film's attacks on the president were in poor taste, conspiracy minded, and largely irrelevant. They dismissed Fahrenheit 9/11 as fiction, not fact. White House communications director Dan Bartlett and radio host Rush Limbaugh briefly summarized the spirit of these complaints. Bartlett said that the movie was "outrageously false," and Limbaugh called it "a pack of lies."[6]

Since complaints about the film's excessive partisanship were central to many critiques, chapter 4 places Moore's oeuvre in a broader context. It examines the evidence of an emerging tradition of a "committed" form of documentary production. There are many approaches to crafting documentaries, and the techniques employed by Michael Moore in Fahrenheit 9/11 resemble those used by earlier artists in important ways. Moore made some imaginative contributions to the genre, but he also profited greatly from the work of documentary pioneers who came before him. This broad view of film history suggests that the term documentary relates to strongly opinionated filmmaking as well as to productions that purport to offer balanced and dispassionate perspectives. Furthermore, I maintain that all documentary filmmaking is a partisan exercise in significant ways, because the production process requires an artist to choose and reject cinematic evidence at every turn.

Did *Fahrenheit 9/11* present and interpret the facts of recent U.S. history, politics, and foreign policy in responsible and sophisticated ways? Did the documentary evidence available to Moore at the time of his movie's production support or contradict the principal arguments he presented? From which sources did Moore draw his "facts"? What did other accomplished documentary filmmakers say about his approach to interpretation? How did Moore defend himself in the face of many pointed criticisms about his use of evidence and his efforts to persuade audiences of his point of view? Was *Fahrenheit 9/11* essentially true or false in its spin on the recent past? These important questions, which were raised frequently in the national media, are the subject of chapter 5. The title of the chapter, "Let the Debate Begin," comes from Moore's statement to the press as he defended his movie against the many challenges to its facts. Moore insisted that he had made a strong case for his interpretation. This chapter considers the debate about *Fahrenheit 9/11* from the perspective of the filmmaker and his supporters.

Chapter 6 deals with a familiar and challenging question: Can a popular and provocative movie make a difference? Does it have the potential to influence public opinion or, more importantly, change it? Michael Moore constructed *Fahrenheit 9/11* with the goal of influencing attitudes. He said, "I believe the film is going to bring hundreds of thousands of people to the polls who otherwise were not going to vote. I think it's going to have a tremendous impact in that way."[7] Moore confessed that his intention was to arouse viewers' emotions. It was not enough just to entertain audiences; Moore wanted them to take action. He said, "My mantra in the editing room has been: We've got to make a movie where, on the way out of the theatre, the people ask the ushers if they have any torches."[8]

Opinions vary greatly on the question of *Fahrenheit 9/11*'s influence on American voters. Some political pundits believe that the film played well with Americans who were already convinced of Michael Moore's point of view. They maintain that most of the people who saw the movie in the summer of 2004 were already disillusioned with Bush's policies and were unlikely to vote for him. Thus, say these pundits, Moore was "preaching to the choir." Conservatives, Republicans, and supporters of the president either viewed the movie with anger or refused to watch it.[9] Some critics, such as *New York Times* columnist David Brooks, claimed that Moore's controversial and sharply partisan film would backfire, alienating many voters. The excitement over *Fahrenheit 9/11*, Brooks predicted, could help President Bush win reelection.

Who was right? Did the film promote discontent with the president's policies, as Michael Moore intended? Did it have a negative impact, inciting many Americans to come to the defense of a supposedly maligned president? Or did the movie have virtually no effect, because only people sympathetic to the filmmaker's perspective took it seriously?

To throw light on some possible answers, chapter 6 reviews data from national opinion polls and the judgments of various observers regarding the movie's influence. The chapter also offers a broader perspective by briefly examining the historical record of popular movies that have dealt with controversial subjects. This analysis places disputes about *Fahrenheit 9/11*'s impact within the context of earlier discussions about cinema's power to move audiences. What does this evidence reveal? Do popular films sometimes affect viewers' attitudes? How are such effects measured? Can movies make a specific impact on viewers' behavior, too? Do films sometimes influence the outcome of elections? These issues are considered in chapter 6 as well.

Debates over the potential impact of *Fahrenheit 9/11* were not an insignificant subsidiary issue; they were central to public disputes about the film's significance. Many Democrats were excited about *Fahrenheit 9/11*'s potential for influencing public opinion and recommended its widest possible distribution. Many Republicans worried that the film could harm the president's reputation at a time when he was engaged in a tight race for reelection. They worked hard to discredit the film's arguments, to marginalize its creator as an extremist, and to pressure theaters to keep the movie off their screens. As the commentary in chapter 6 demonstrates, the stakes appeared to be tremendously important at the time of the film's release. In this sense, *Fahrenheit 9/11* represents an interesting test case for discussing the potential influence of politically oriented movies on national opinion.

Although various groups tried to discredit *Fahrenheit 9/11* and prevent its screening, Disney's decision that its subsidiary, Miramax, should not release the film does not belong with these other examples of obstructionism. Moore complained that Disney president Michael Eisner had blocked the release of *Fahrenheit 9/11* because the movie was politically sensitive. Moore suggested that his film would anger Florida governor Jeb Bush (the president's brother), which might endanger tax breaks for Disney's theme parks in the Sunshine State. However, Disney had stepped away from the distribution of other controversial Miramax films, such as *Priest* and *Dogma*. Deals with other distributors had allowed those films to be shown, and similar deals were struck for *Fahrenheit 9/11*. In view of the potential impact of Moore's movie on the 2004 presidential election, the timidity of Disney's corporate leaders was not particularly surprising. Ironically, the actions of Eisner and other Disney executives probably served the interests of *Fahrenheit 9/11*'s creator. Moore may have promoted the notion of in-house censorship on Disney's part to gain valuable publicity when his movie hit the theaters.[10]

The conclusion compares Michael Moore's message in *Fahrenheit 9/11* with interpretations delivered in the same year by two distinguished commentators on U.S. politics: historian Arthur Schlesinger Jr. and Senator Robert C. Byrd. While Moore communicated his viewpoints through the medium of an entertaining film, Schlesinger and Byrd reviewed the recent past through fact-laden books that sharply criticized the policies of the Bush administration. Moore and the two authors approached history with strikingly different tools, yet in fundamental ways they based their cases on similar evidence and drew related conclusions. These similarities bear directly on the basic questions addressed in this book about the integrity of *Fahrenheit 9/11*'s depiction of events.

1 The Reel Politics of Michael Moore

In 1989 a Flint, Michigan, native who had never made a film before and claimed that he had never earned more than $15,000 a year signed a contract to distribute his new movie through Warner Brothers. The deal was worth $3 million in an "up-front" payment. The young man's inexpensively constructed film quickly became a hit. Initial screenings at film festivals in the United States and Canada elicited standing ovations and considerable buzz about a likely Academy Award nomination. Major film societies in Los Angeles and New York identified Michael Moore's film as the best documentary of the year. Once this motion picture reached American neighborhoods, it quickly accumulated more cash from ticket sales than any other documentary film ever produced in the United States.

Michael Moore's movie *Roger & Me* sharply criticized General Motors, one of the nation's largest corporations. It attacked the company for laying off thousands of autoworkers in Flint, Michigan. The hard-hitting film pleased many viewers, who praised it as an entertaining documentary that also managed to raise important social and political questions. Yet it also became the object of angry criticism. Some called *Roger & Me* a highly distorted and untruthful interpretation of events in Flint. All this praise and condemnation lifted the film's creator from obscurity to fame in just a few weeks. Moore, a chubby thirty-five-year-old who had recently experienced disappointments in his professional career, was suddenly very successful and very controversial.

The story of Michael Moore's good fortune and problems when marketing *Roger & Me* is closely related to the record of his progress and difficulties when distributing and promoting *Fahrenheit 9/11*. By 2004, Moore had become more sophisticated as a filmmaker and an activist, but in essential ways he was still the same cinematic gadfly he had been in 1989. An examination of the brouhaha surrounding *Roger & Me* serves, then, as useful introduction to the nature of the debates that animated Americans when *Fahrenheit 9/11* reached the theaters. Arguments about *Roger & Me*'s treatment of evidence resembled the debates years later about *Fahrenheit 9/11*. Indeed, similar arguments turned up in response to two other movies by Michael Moore, *The Big One* (1997) and *Bowling for Columbine* (2002). In each case, the filmmaker defended his production vigorously, and critics lambasted him for taking too many liberties.

The debates over these films looked, at first glance, like disagreements about standards in documentary filmmaking, but there were important political subtexts to the clashes. Conflicting opinions did not reflect merely different ideas about artistic concepts such as camera work, interviewing, and editing. Often, the disputes related to contemporary messages embedded in the movies. Individuals who agreed with those messages tended to praise Moore for constructing an impressive film. Those who disagreed with his interpretations tended to disparage the film on artistic grounds, concentrating on its cinematic techniques rather than directly disputing the filmmaker's economic and political arguments.

No documentary filmmaker has been more successful than Moore in provoking public discussions about economics and politics. And no filmmaker has aroused as much negative sentiment as Moore has. On many occasions Moore has confessed that he wants his movies to make audiences think and act. His productions have certainly functioned in that way by arousing both intense support and opposition to his causes.

How did Michael Moore's early life experiences influence his political perspectives as a filmmaker? What were his principal purposes in making *Roger & Me*? Which distinctive cinematic strategies did he bring to his project, and why did his filmmaking become so controversial? Why did intense debate continue to surround Moore's work as he engaged in other film and book projects? The record of Moore's personal and professional experiences prior to 2004 provides a useful context for understanding the confrontations between Moore and his critics over *Fahrenheit 9/11*.

Michael Moore lacked knowledge about filmmaking before he began working on *Roger & Me*, but he was certainly familiar with the problems of blue-collar workers in the auto plants of Flint, Michigan. Moore's father had worked at GM's A. C. Spark Plug division for more than three decades before *Roger & Me* reached the theaters. His uncle had participated in the famous 1937 sit-down strike at a GM plant in Flint that had helped establish the United Auto Workers (UAW) as a strong bargaining agent for workers in the auto industry. His family eventually moved out of Flint and into the white, middle-class community of Davison. Like many children of GM employees, Michael Moore expected to pursue a career in the factories, but he made a fateful decision one day that changed his life dramatically. After graduating from high school, Moore obtained a job on GM's assembly line. The morning he was to begin work at the GM factory, he heard his father preparing to leave for work and felt a sense of panic, imagining that he too could spend the rest of his working days on the assembly line. He chose to stay home and give up a job that many young men of Flint would have been happy to take.

Moore came from a rather humble background, but he showed early signs of restiveness, independence, and ambition. He had studied at a Catholic seminary in Saginaw during his high school years and considered becoming a priest, but that notion quickly passed. Nevertheless, as he explained years later, his time at the seminary had left him thinking that "I should be doing something with my life that benefits society."[1] He recalled the power of that religious training, saying, "in my head I never left the seminary."[2] As a young man, Moore began to exhibit leadership qualities. He achieved the rank of Eagle Scout and distinguished himself as the class clown in high school activities. When the United States lowered the voting age, Moore ran for public office in his community and at age eighteen became one of the youngest public servants in the nation. At the time, he exhibited greater political awareness than many other teenagers. His two sisters had taken him on trips to Washington and talked at length about the workings of government. In the late 1960s, controversies over the Vietnam War both fascinated and troubled him.

Displaying an interest in journalism, Moore embarked on a career that quickly distinguished him as an innovator and as a young man with strong political opinions. After dropping out of the University of Michigan during his first year, Moore started an alternative newspaper called the *Flint Voice* at age twenty-two. That little periodical proved successful and eventually took on the broader title of the *Michigan Voice*. Moore's editorship of the spunky *Voice* helped him secure a coveted position in San Francisco as the executive editor of *Mother Jones*, a prominent left-wing magazine. At that point his career in journalism seemed to be taking off, but it quickly came to a stop. After a few months on the job at *Mother Jones*, Moore got into an argument with his associates over political matters. He refused to sanction the publication of an article that was highly critical of the left-wing Sandinista regime in Nicaragua (which he admired), and he was fired. Later, Moore sued *Mother Jones* for $2 million and received an out-of-court settlement of

$58,000. The check did not diminish his pain from the experience, how-ever. Feeling depressed and uncertain about his next move, Moore returned to his native Flint in 1986.[3]

Although Michael Moore often sounded like a radical lefty during those days, his thinking took many directions, and he did not clearly identify with any ideological position. At times he articulated concepts of the New Left that had emerged in the late 1960s and early 1970s. He spoke harshly of capitalism and hinted that something "different" might work better. When describing the purpose of his first movie, Moore said, "I wanted the ugly underpinnings of our economic system exposed," and about the problems of Flint, Michigan, he said, "Until you have a different system you will have Flints."[4] But how different would that different system have to be? Moore was not clear. He often claimed that he was fundamentally confident that the United States' major problems could be corrected once the people rec-ognized them and committed themselves to changing conditions. "I'm generally an optimistic person," he told the press. "I believe that eventually people do the right thing. But it takes a while sometimes."[5] Despite Moore's many comments expressing frustration with the way capitalism worked, he acted more like a reformer who wanted to make the free-enterprise system serve the people better than a Marxist who wished to destroy capitalism and replace it with something radically different.

Finding a personal mission seemed to be a good way to get over his fir-ing from Mother Jones, and Moore soon discovered just such a remedy. His arrival back in Flint came at a troublesome time for the city. There had been several plant closings, firings, and layoffs at the various GM facilities. Unem-ployment in Flint had grown to 26 percent, one of the highest jobless rates in the country. The city looked poor, too. By the 1980s, there were many aban-doned and dilapidated commercial buildings and houses around town. Hun-dreds of Flint citizens whose families had lived and worked in the community for decades were moving to the South or the West. General Motors, which had dominated the local economy for years, was planning to hire laborers for manufacturing plants in Mexico, where wages were much lower.

Here was an important news story that had attractive possibilities for a populist-minded journalist. Moore could focus on Flint's problems, and the town's difficulties could stand in for the much broader problems facing many Rust Belt communities in the northern states. There was an emerg-ing pattern of economic troubles: corporations were downsizing or closing down manufacturing facilities and moving production to countries with a cheaper labor force. Moore sensed that a commentary on Flint's problems could serve as an allegory. His study could cite Flint as a severe example of the hardships that were troubling blue-collar workers all over the United States. Moore intended to argue that the corporate executives' hunger for profits was leading them to abandon American employees and the communities they lived in. A report on Flint's problems represented a broader tragedy that was occurring across the land.[6] He could have leveled similar charges against leaders at Lockheed, General Electric, or U.S. Steel, Moore once told the press. His target was General Motors because he was familiar with the situation in Flint. "I just happened to be born in Flint to a man who worked in the shop," he explained.[7]

Michael Moore wanted to do more than just make audiences think about the problems of the declining industrial areas of the country. He intended to shake them up and inspire them to *do something* about the situation. Film seemed like an attractive medium for arousing such emotions, and Moore created *Roger & Me* and his later movies with this action-oriented goal in mind. He thought that cinema was more likely to provoke the masses into action than were the print media, noting that film also had the potential to reach much larger audiences than an article or a book could. When explaining his filmmaking purpose during a promotion tour for *Roger & Me*, he said, "I want people to be angry; I want them to get up and do something."[8] The film should not leave audiences in despair, he stated, because "despair is paralyzing." Anger would serve better to excite demands for reform, and film could best stimulate that sense of outrage and the determination to correct what was wrong.[9]

Michael Moore believed that traditional news reporting on television and traditional documentary filmmaking were not much better than books in arousing people to action. Newscasts and documentaries usually failed to awaken audiences emotionally or stir them to get involved in politics. He felt that the national news media had not done enough to incite feelings of rage about the plight of industrial workers and the impact of layoffs on American communities. To provoke strong interest in these problems, his film would need to deliver images that were quite different from the ones typically seen on the six o'clock news. Shots of unemployment lines were too familiar and boring, he thought.[10] A truly provocative film would have to tell the story of workers' troubles in a distinctive manner. He did not intend to produce "another dying-steel-town, dying-auto-town documentary." Those depressing reports did not resonate with viewers, Moore said. "They're boring. They're paralyzing."[11]

Nor did Michael Moore want to construct a film that would appeal only to the left-wing, documentary-loving, art-house "ghetto." He did not wish to produce "a conventional documentary full of statistics" that made viewers want to leave the theater or grab the remote-control device to switch the channel. His motion picture needed to be more broadly entertaining so that it could appeal to diverse audiences. "We need more documentaries made by people who hate documentaries," he suggested.[12]

Moore intended to present a picture that the national news had not delivered. When he spoke publicly about the work of people in the television news media, Moore sometimes sounded contemptuous. At one point during the promotion of *Roger & Me*, he asserted brashly, "When the media starts doing their job, I go back to my Tostidos and dip."[13] Years later, when speaking about *Fahrenheit 9/11*, Moore offered similarly contemptuous remarks about the news media. In 2004 he said, "I'm an overweight white guy in a baseball cap who doesn't even have a college education and is uncovering things they aren't."[14] Such confrontational statements about the supposed shortcomings of TV journalists communicated a central thesis in Moore's cinema. The filmmaker wanted to tell stories that network news organizations were unwilling to take on directly and forthrightly. He maintained that network executives were too timid to take strong stands, and their reporters imitated their example, for fear of alienating advertisers and viewers. Moore intended to handle stories with controversial political implications much less cautiously than the networks had done.

Michael Moore's protests against the timidity of the news media gave his films an unusual punch, but they also incited the anger of powerful figures in the print and video-based professions. Every time Moore criticized newspeople for failing to perform their jobs aggressively, some journalists struck back sharply. His tendency to chastise print and television journalists for failing to raise tough questions excited intense wrath from many professionals. When *Roger & Me* and *Fahrenheit 9/11* became controversial, quite a few prominent figures in the national news media joined forces with the critics who slammed Moore's films for ideological reasons. Hence, Moore grabbed public attention by pointing to the news media's shortcomings, but his actions also risked alienating prominent individuals who would turn against his work.

When constructing *Roger & Me*, Moore intended to design a film that incorporated a good deal of humor to make his strong messages more palatable. He wanted to make viewers laugh as well as cry, smile as well as get angry. Moore sensed that levity would keep audiences watching his picture and absorbing its lessons, whereas a totally serious movie seemed unlikely to hold viewers' attention and arouse their interest over a two-hour period. Moviegoers were unlikely to watch a long and tedious documentary about the woes of Flint. Moore would need to entertain them, and his old antics as class clown could facilitate that effort. The Left, he thought, often failed to understand the potential of humor to get important points across. If Moore intended to succeed in influencing behavior, he needed to construct a film that would appeal to more than just the art-house crowd and the nation's liberal intellectuals. Moore hoped to make an amusing and entertaining film, yet one that was also thought-provoking. He wanted to design a movie that many Americans would watch in their local theaters—"to enjoy with Goobers," as he put it.[15]

A number of film reviewers judged him successful in eliciting laughter while presenting powerful social commentary. Vincent Canby of the *New York Times* called Moore a modern-day Mark Twain, and the *Nation's* David Corn compared the documentary filmmaker to Charlie Chaplin.[16] Moore especially liked the latter comparison, because Chaplin was a genius at using comedy to make social commentary.[17] At various times Moore identified his oeuvre as "docucomedy" or "mockumentary."[18] Some commentators in the media referred to him as the "Woody Allen of documentary films."[19]

When Michael Moore began making *Roger & Me*, he received valuable assistance from two artists who had made important contributions to the development of committed documentary production in the United States: Kevin Rafferty and Anne Bohlen. Moore needed their assistance because in the early days, as he said, he did not know the difference between an "f-stop and a truck stop."[20] Rafferty had been a key figure in the making of the funny but powerfully critical *Atomic Café*, and Bohlen had helped create *With Babies and Banners* (1978), an examination of women's roles in the famous Flint auto workers' strike of 1937. Both Rafferty and Bohlen worked with Moore in Flint, giving him a crash course in filmmaking. Rafferty stayed with the project and served as a principal cameraman for *Roger & Me*.

Kevin Rafferty had first met Michael Moore at an outdoor café in the Soho section of New York City, where the two talked about the challenges of raising funds for moviemaking. Rafferty revealed that he was working on a film about right-wing militia members in the United States, and Moore gave him a lead on a Michigan group with which he was familiar. The two men became friends, and Rafferty gave Moore a part in his documentary *Blood in the Face*. In one notable scene Moore interviews a blonde woman in a Nazi uniform and cleverly elicits comments by casually remarking that she seems out of place because she is good-looking enough to be in a television commercial. Moore seemed pleased with his performance, and the experience may have given him the notion that he could achieve his political purposes by appearing on-camera in his own films.[21]

Obtaining the $160,000 to make *Roger & Me* presented a substantial challenge to the young and inexperienced filmmaker. Moore combined funds from a number of different sources to get the project into production. He raised about $50,000 by creating a weekly bingo game in Flint and also used funds from his *Mother Jones* settlement. Moore sold his home in Flint to raise additional money, and he took financial commitments from various Michigan friends and residents.[22] Eventually enough cash flowed into his account to cover expenses for the two and a half years of filming and editing, and production work ended in August 1989.

When Moore secured the deal with Warner Brothers, he did not simply pocket all the money. The arrangement with Warner included some unusual terms. The filmmaker required Warner Brothers to avoid screening the movie in nonunion cinemas. From the profits, $25,000 would be used to pay rent for the families depicted in the movie as victims of eviction. Warner Brothers also agreed to issue 20,000 movie tickets to unemployed Americans living throughout the country, and the movie was to be shown free of charge in labor halls in fifty American cities. Money was also set aside to send a small group of Moore's associates to these screenings, where they would lead union members in public discussions of the relevant issues, including corporate responsibility. Additionally, Moore channeled 40 percent of the earnings from *Roger & Me* to a nonprofit foundation designed to help finance the work of other first-time filmmakers.[23]

Roger & Me, like many successful film narratives, focuses on personalities. Moore's movie draws particular attention to two individuals—one who is quite visible, one who is invisible. Moore himself is a distinctive presence in the film, and often a comic one. He appears in various scenes with ruffled hair, jeans, a sportsman's shirt, and a windbreaker. The inscription on his baseball cap says, "I'm Out for Trout." In several scenes he has a toothpick dangling from his mouth. Moore is the main on-screen character who ties the various stories together. Roger Smith, the chairman of General Motors, is the invisible one. Moore engages in a seemingly endless and totally frustrating pursuit of the head of GM. He tells viewers that he wants to meet Roger Smith and ask him to come to Flint so that he can tour the devastation that has been caused, in large part, because of the recent layoffs at GM plants. It seems obvious that the powerful corporate executive will not accept this offer from an obscure young man and his production crew armed with microphones and cameras. Moore's search is really a stunt, and a clever one. It is a dramatic device that gives the movie comic relief and illustrates the filmmaker's argument that corporate leaders are indifferent to the concerns of the public.

In one particularly humorous moment in the movie, Moore enters GM headquarters in Detroit, and a security guard asks for the filmmaker's business card. Moore does not have one, so he hands the man an identification card from Chuck E. Cheese (a restaurant popular with children). As reviewer John Hartl noted, Moore delivered an important message by putting himself into the story and showing how difficult it was to get a word with the business leader who had taken jobs from the people of Flint. Michael Moore, said Hartl, "is standing in for anyone who's ever been thwarted by an executive who didn't return phone calls or a secretary who behaved like a security guard."[24]

This mixture of levity and seriousness continues unabated throughout the movie. Moore shows that the people of Flint are struggling to make ends meet, but he also illustrates their resourcefulness in finding ways to earn money while they are unemployed. One case involves a woman who raises and sells rabbits in her backyard. The bunnies are available, she announces, for "pets or meat," and she expertly kills one. Some of the other examples seem even more tragic, as in the case of a man who sells his blood.

In Moore's first movie, and in his subsequent films, attention to class issues is evident throughout. *Roger & Me* deals with the wealth gap by juxtaposing scenes of the hardscrabble lives of everyday citizens and the privileged, comfortable lives of Michigan's wealthy elite. Moore reveals that some of the unemployed citizens take jobs as "living statues" for a *Great Gatsby* costume party. At a benefit to raise funds for a newly opened prison, wealthy guests are "booked" and "imprisoned" for the evening. Moore searches for Roger Smith in favorite haunts of the rich and locally important, such as the Detroit Athletic Club and the Grosse Point Yacht Club. He concludes the movie with a striking juxtaposition of power and powerlessness: scenes of Smith's inspirational Christmas speech to company managers and their families are mixed with scenes filmed the same evening of a Flint family being evicted for nonpayment of rent—their furniture, a Christmas tree, and other personal belongings deposited outside.

In addition to the emotion-packed finish, which has become a trademark of Michael Moore's documentaries, *Roger & Me* features another technique that has become familiar: scenes that make the rich and powerful look superficial and silly. Moore lets these figures sully their reputations through their own words and actions. Most notably, he focuses on the efforts of Flint's political leaders to give their economically troubled city a happy face. The leaders bring notables to Flint to offer inspiring messages. Evangelist Robert Schuller comes to town briefly and offers a positive thought, saying, "Change your hurt into a halo." Anita Bryant, a familiar spokesperson for Florida orange juice, announces, "Today is a new day." Pop singer Pat Boone reports that GM's leader, Roger Smith, is a "can-do kind of guy." Ronald Reagan (in video footage from a 1980 campaign tour) takes unemployed workers out for pizza and suggests that they move to Texas to find work. Additionally, Moore reports on Flint leaders' expensive efforts to revive the city through construction of a new Hyatt-Regency hotel, a new downtown shoppers' pavilion, and a theme park called Autoworld. The three business enterprises failed, Moore indicates, at considerable cost to the city's taxpayers.

In a pattern somewhat similar to the public reactions to *Fahrenheit 9/11*, *Roger & Me* received acclaim at first but then quickly came under intense attack from commentators who disapproved of the filmmaker's message and techniques. In many cases, the detractors disapproved of Moore himself.

The initial success of *Roger & Me* at the film festivals alerted movie critics to its importance. A number of generally positive reviews appeared in the press and on television during the picture's first days of distribution. Then came an onslaught of hostile reactions. Critics lashed out at the movie in the national media, and before long, this professional bad-mouthing made a significant impact. Even though *Roger & Me* initially looked like a shoo-in for an Academy Award nomination for best documentary, the many well-circulated negative comments about supposed violations of standards in documentary filmmaking undermined the production's reputation. When the Academy of Motion Picture Arts and Sciences counted the votes, *Roger & Me* had not received a nomination, despite being the most financially successful documentary film in U.S. history. This result brought a reaction from some Hollywood professionals. A group of forty-five prominent figures, including several past Oscar winners and nominees, sent an "Open Letter to the Film Community" to protest the activities of the Documentary Screening Committee that had made the selections for best documentary.[25]

Four film reviews and commentaries contributed most significantly to the public downgrading of *Roger & Me*'s reputation, each of which received considerable attention in the national media. The first bombshell appeared in the November–December issue of *Film Comment*. Harlan Jacobson featured an interview with Moore, who admitted to rearranging the chronological sequence of some historical events in his presentation. Pauline Kael followed with a detailed critique of *Roger & Me* in the *New Yorker* that charged the filmmaker with violating traditional standards of documentary production. Her most-quoted observation was a characterization of the movie as "shallow and facetious, a piece of gonzo demagoguery that made me feel cheap for laughing."[26] Additionally, David Bensman, a university professor, wrote a commentary on the film for the *New York Times* that featured an extremely damning title: "*Roger & Me*: Narrow, Simplistic, Wrong." Then John Harkness published a stinging review in *Sight and Sound* that reiterated some of the previous criticisms and blasted Moore for acting like a prima donna.

All four of these writers demonstrated a rather limited appreciation of the style of documentary production that Michael Moore was undertaking. The critics appeared uncomfortable with Moore's highly personal approach to cinematic presentation. They showed little tolerance for his mixture of serious and humorous material, and they considered his unorthodox editing techniques disturbing. The critics accused Moore of manipulating evidence and, essentially, distorting the historical record. These detractors tended to praise traditional techniques of documentary production and looked askance at Moore's flamboyant and sharply opinionated artistic style. In many ways, their reactions approximated the responses to *Fahrenheit 9/11* a decade and a half later.

Harlan Jacobson's case against Moore came in the form of a hostile interview. Jacobson essentially ambushed Moore, firing pointed questions at him in a way that produced a tense verbal exchange. Jacobson maintained that Moore presented historical information out of sequence in *Roger & Me*. The interviewer called these sequential matters "disquieting discrepancies." He noted, for example, that Ronald Reagan had visited Flint in 1980 as a presidential candidate, not later in the decade after the big layoffs had occurred at General Motors. Furthermore, the cash register that Moore claimed was stolen during Reagan's visit was actually the object of criminal action two days later (Moore subsequently proved that the store owner had told him incorrectly that the theft occurred on the same day). Jacobson noted that GM plant closings took place over several years, not in one big blow that sent shock waves over Flint. The interviewer also observed that Flint leaders and a charitable foundation supported the failed hotel, theme park, and pavilion *before* the major layoffs at General Motors. Other reviewers, such as Gary Crowdus of *Cineaste*, accepted Moore's simplification of this story, noting that *Roger & Me* was correct in its basic message: there had been ill-considered and wasteful spending of public funds in Flint.[27] Jacobson, however, allowed the filmmaker no latitude in the matter. He charged Moore with fudging details. Jacobson suggested that Moore deliberately left the impression that all these events had occurred after General Motors laid off thousands of workers. The reviewer treated these matters as egregious mistakes. A documentary film, he asserted, should not "screw around" with sequences.[28]

Jacobson's nagging about sequences and dates was essentially unfair, because neither Moore nor the film actually said what Jacobson claimed they did. As Crowdus pointed out in his lengthy discussion of the film, Moore shows a clip of Dan Rather of CBS News (not Moore, at this point) announcing the statistics regarding plant closings and lost jobs, and other numbers are mentioned in various segments of the film. "This phony debate about numbers shouldn't obscure the film's illustration of the devastating ripple effect of GM's action," wrote Crowdus.[29]

Many commentators in the national media cited Jacobson's interview as a stunning revelation of Michael Moore's flaws. They pointed to Jacobson's discoveries of compromised chronologies and claimed that the newly popular filmmaker was, essentially, trying to sell the public phony goods. Yet the opinion writers who gave credence to Jacobson's claims of slaying a newly arrived dragon fed lavishly by big cash from Hollywood tended to overlook Moore's perceptive observations in response to Jacobson's questions and arguments. In the exchanges, Moore took a modern, innovative approach to the interpretation of political issues in film. In contrast, Jacobson pursued an old-fashioned approach, trapped in a traditional vision of the way documentaries should be constructed. He seemed incapable of imagining the evolutionary and revolutionary possibilities of the art form.

Moore repeatedly told the interviewer that all journalism involves some manipulation of sequences, and in fact, journalists edit all the time— taking out some information and putting other information in. Moore never intended to offer a strict, chronological, historical report on developments in Flint, he said. "The movie is about essentially what happened to the town during the 1980s," he explained, and it was honest in its basic depiction. "I was true to what happened," he affirmed. "Everything that happened in the movie happened." Moore maintained that he could not include all the information that Jacobson wanted, such as numerical details and dates. If he had tried to do so, *Roger & Me* would have been a three-hour film, didactic and boring. A traditional educational approach would have failed dismally as a theatrical production.

Each time Jacobson insisted that *Roger & Me* was a documentary and that its creator must be held accountable to the standards of documentary filmmaking, Moore replied that it was, instead, a "movie"—and an entertaining one at that. When Jacobson called for greater presentation of historical information in the film, Moore protested, "You are holding me to a different standard than you would another film as if I were writing some kind of college essay." At one point in the interview, Jacobson argued that Moore should have placed an insert or a crawl in *Roger & Me* to give viewers specific information about General Motors' downsizing activities over a span of eight years. Moore replied that Jacobson was expecting a year-by-year historical report, which was not his intent. When Jacobson asked why Moore had failed to include detailed information about contributions by the Charles Stewart Mott Foundation toward improvements in Flint, Moore explained that although the inclusion of that fact and other historical details might be appropriate for an article, it was not appropriate for his film. Facts about the Mott Foundation's work in Flint did not appear in *Roger & Me* because, Moore stressed, "I was making a movie."[30]

Despite Moore's repeated invitations to Jacobson to think open-mindedly about the production's style and message, the interviewer remained caught up in his limited vision of a documentary film's capacity to stir the thinking of audiences. The interviewer insisted that Moore's movie should have taken a more traditional approach to the presentation of historical facts. When Moore would not agree, Jacobson asked, "Are you talking about a fiction film or a documentary?" A documentary film, Jacobson suggested, was essentially either true or false, and Moore's extensive use of artistic license seemed to earn his movie a charge of falsehood.

Pauline Kael, noted film analyst for the *New Yorker*, mentioned the Jacobson article in her review, and familiarity with that report evidently colored her reaction to *Roger & Me*. Kael described some of the charges that Jacobson had leveled concerning the sequence of historical events in Flint. She complained, too, that Moore often gave his story a comic feel at the expense of the good citizens of Michigan. Moore's camera made "brutal fun of people," she complained; it characterized the leaders of Flint as "incompetent twerps," and it made the common folk look silly. Audiences could laugh at them yet still feel that they were being politically correct, she observed. Moore was "too glib" and presented stories "in cartoon form" like a "slick ad executive," Kael complained.[31] His message was also much too simplistic, because it made the problems in Flint appear to be entirely the fault of GM chairman Roger Smith.

Kael was one of the country's most acclaimed film analysts at the time, but her discussion of *Roger & Me* revealed a limited understanding of the new art form that Michael Moore was developing. Much too readily, she dismissed the humorous content in Moore's work as superficial and meaningless rather than recognizing that it served a serious purpose. Moore gave his movie levity to draw the audience's attention to the problems that troubled him. Nevertheless, Kael anticipated a common complaint voiced about Moore's other movies, especially *Fahrenheit 9/11*. Moore's critics often spoke angrily of his efforts to elicit laughs from the comments of American citizens, poor and rich. They claimed that Moore often took these quotes out of context and essentially used them to ridicule the speakers. Through careful editing techniques, they said, Moore tended to make his on-camera subjects sound like jerks.

The third notable salvo fired against Moore's film came from David Bensman, chairman of the Labor Education Department at Rutgers University. Bensman published a scathing commentary about *Roger & Me* in the *New York Times*. He charged that the movie's principal thesis was wrong, because leaders at General Motors were not insensitive to the needs of their workers. In fact, corporate managers had embarked on a multibillion-dollar plan to make the Michigan plants more technologically sophisticated. These reforms applied to facilities in Flint as well, Bensman noted. "The story of Flint's ruination is much more complicated than Mr. Moore's explanation of GM's arrogance and indifference to the working class," he insisted. Like Kael, Bensman also registered complaints about the way *Roger & Me* depicted the common people. Moore portrayed them as victims, argued Bensman, even though many citizens of Flint had lobbied local and national leaders to provide help to the community and had run for public office in efforts to improve their situation.[32]

Bensman, like several other commentators who criticized Moore for not addressing the causes of Flint's problems, failed to acknowledge that a provocative documentary often raises more questions than it answers. Moore's purpose was to arouse audience sympathy for the plight of the region's blue-collar workers, including the newly unemployed. He was not attempting to provide a textbook-length review of the diverse historic causes of worker layoffs in Flint. As he had told Harlan Jacobson in the interview for *Film Comment*, "It's a movie, you know; you can't do everything." Bensman's commentary on the history of GM's relations with its workers was actually a useful response to the movie. It exemplified Moore's goal of encouraging Americans to talk about the relevant issues in public forums. Ironically, Bensman's arguments could be held up to illustrate that *Roger & Me* was, indeed, arousing interest in the problems of Flint, as Moore had wanted from the beginning.

The fourth sharply critical reaction appeared in a review by John Harkness in the respected film magazine *Sight and Sound*. Harkness's review also mentioned the discrepancies reported in Jacobson's interview, but Harkness objected more to the filmmaker's style of presentation than his manipulation of chronology. Harkness expressed disapproval of Moore's efforts to place himself at the center of the action in *Roger & Me*. The reviewer argued that Moore was attempting to be a Capraesque figure, a hero of the common folk who fought boldly for their interests against wealthy, powerful, and influential figures. Moore portrayed Michigan society in the fashion of Frank Capra, showing divisions between rapacious and indifferent rich people and the humble and suffering little folks. Roger Smith served as the villain in this drama, much like Edward Arnold had played the gold-plated heavy in Capra's movies of the 1930s and 1940s, and Moore resembled the Jimmy Stewart character in Capra's classic *Mr. Smith Goes to Washington* (1939). Moore took on the role of bold defender of the common people, driven by his messianic impulses. There was little complexity in the simplistic plot, Harkness complained. No wealthy Michigan citizens appcarcd in thc movie to express concern about the troubles in Flint. Where, Harkness asked, were "the articulate union members, the community organizers, the people who fought the plant closings?" They were absent, Harkness argued, because Michael Moore wanted "to be in sole possession of the truth."[33]

Harkness treated Moore as a scene-grabber, an egotistical and power-hungry artist who enjoyed manipulating his image and his movie's reporting in order to gain fame and fortune. The filmmaker presented himself to audiences as an "aw-shucks kind of guy" who seemed not to know what he was doing, but this supposedly folksy fellow was actually an experienced and hard-edged journalist. Furthermore, Moore's central theme in *Roger & Me* was phony, the critic observed, because "everything about the film suggests that the last thing [Moore] wanted was an interview with Roger Smith." Surely, Harkness argued, Moore knew that he would need proper press credentials to get an interview with the GM leader, and as a former magazine publisher and commentator on National Public Radio, Moore could have easily obtained the necessary documents.

Harkness also blasted the moviemaker for making entertainment more important than the issues. Moore focused on personal stories rather than the broad social and economic forces that affected industrial workers, Harkness noted, and the filmmaker limited himself "to the death of one town and actions of one company easily personified by its chief executive officer." This highly critical reviewer could not resist taking a personal shot at Moore, too, for signing a $3 million deal to distribute his movie. Warner Brothers was part of Time Warner, the largest entertainment conglomerate in the world, noted Harkness. What an interesting development in the life of a populist who enjoyed criticizing corporate capitalism![34]

Of course, a defender of innovative cinema could easily praise Michael Moore for employing the very techniques that Harkness criticized. The elements in *Roger & Me* that troubled Harkness were important dramatic strategies that Moore used intelligently to make his movie appealing, and these strategies involved exercises in artistic license. By appearing frequently on-camera and at the center of the story, Moore gave personality and humor to his narration. Rather than featuring the familiar unseen and apparently omniscient narrator, Moore brought himself into the story and accented the notion that his film represented a highly personal and opinionated essay. His Capraesque approach to storytelling nicely served the goal of stirring audience sympathies for the working-class victims in Flint. Wealthy auto executives and town leaders featured on-screen were indeed simplistic heavies in a carefully planned dramatic design, but Moore's suggestions about the clash of class and cultural interests in Michigan helped communicate his thesis forcefully. Moore confessed in the interview with Jacobson that he had simplified and dramatized reality to a certain degree, and he believed that those artistic decisions had been instrumental in taking the motion picture beyond the art houses and into the neighborhood theaters.

In other interviews, Moore suggested that the case of Roger Smith and the plants in Flint served as allegory. Moore's cameras were pointed toward a particular city and a particular corporate leader, but the larger purpose of the movie was to make Americans think about the broader problems associated with changes in manufacturing that affected blue-collar workers everywhere.

Roger & Me began to look vulnerable after the critiques of Jacobson, Kael, Bensman, and Harkness. Soon many other critics joined the fray. The Chicago Tribune's reviewer, Dave Kehr, compared Moore to Hitler's propagandist Leni Riefenstahl.[35] Another commentator charged Moore with presenting "socialistic rhetoric."[36] Nigel Andrews, writing in the Financial Times of London, declared that "'Roger & Me' is the work of a snake-oil salesman with a sense of humor, passing himself off as a qualified doctor." Moore illustrated some problems in Flint, stated Andrews, but he did not make an honest attempt to locate the principal causes of the city's troubles.[37]

Even some generally supportive analysts registered some poignant complaints. Writing in Cineaste, for example, Gary Crowdus noted that Roger & Me lacked the kind of useful contextual information and analysis that good documentaries ought to provide. Crowdus lamented that Moore did not focus "a little more on 'Roger' and somewhat less on 'Me.'"[38] He berated Moore for failing to inform audiences adequately about the history of GM's troubles and pointed out that the automobile company was guilty of questionable activities that had received no attention in the movie. For example, Roger & Me failed to tell viewers that Smith had successfully lobbied the Reagan administration to halt new regulations concerning fuel efficiency, pollution, and safety devices. GM also squeezed out big tax rebates, observed Crowdus, and the powerful company pressed for wage concessions from the UAW at the same time that its executives received pay bonuses.[39] Moore overlooked these important details in an effort to tell his story in a highly personalized way.

As in the case of other critics who had called for more information, Moore had already articulated the proper response. Roger & Me was a movie, not a comprehensive report on the many significant issues surrounding GM policies. But by publishing details about these other topics, Cineaste's editors were actually promoting the kind of dialogue that Moore had encouraged. The filmmaker had hoped to provoke discussion, and the remarks by Crowdus were supportive of that continuing dialogue on the relevant issues.

Some of that lively public debate involved a spirited defense of General

Motors and its policies. For instance, David Whiteside, publisher of the *Power Report*, defended GM and the executives who had received bonuses while many workers were receiving pink slips. "Ask yourself, what's going to contribute to the long-term viability of the company?" Whiteside stated. "Is it withholding executive bonuses for one year or dealing with the fundamental cost issues in its production system?" For Whiteside, layoffs were an unfortunate but necessary development in the company's efforts to modernize and remain competitive. Chester Burger, writing in the *Public Relations Journal*, joined this effort to defend GM. He declared Moore's film "unfair and untruthful" in its depiction of GM's policies and practices. *Roger & Me* blamed Roger Smith for problems that were beyond his control, argued Burger. Broad economic developments forced the company to make changes in its manufacturing practices, he said, yet it had spent a great deal of money to modernize obsolete facilities, including $475 million to make capital improvements in the Flint, Michigan, plants.[40] Interestingly, some UAW leaders and members joined these commentators in defending General Motors. A few of them worried that *Roger & Me*'s indictment of an American automobile company might cause thousands of Americans to buy Toyotas rather than GM products.[41] Other union figures were upset because Moore's film characterized UAW president Owen W. Bieber as a close ally of GM management. The movie implied that Bieber had shown insufficient concern about major layoffs at the plants.

Some people, evidently associated with the union, arranged for Pauline Kael's scathing review to be distributed at public meetings in Michigan where Moore appeared to promote his film. Moore protested these actions, complaining, "There are too many union guys that are friends with management."[42] Of course, not all people in the unions agreed with the anti-Moore perspective. Dave Yettaw, a militant branch leader of Local 599 of the UAW, supported Moore's claim that organized labor showed a tendency to let management into its bedroom.[43]

Ralph Nader, who might have been expected to defend the populist filmmaker, also joined the chorus of criticism, but for different reasons. Nader did not like the way Michael Moore monopolized the spotlight. Nader's associate James Musselman, a Philadelphia lawyer, complained that the movie glorified Moore while "forgetting about all the middle-of-the-road people who worked so hard on these issues and don't get credit."[44] Nader and his colleagues were also troubled because, prior to the film's release, they had published a book that was sharply critical of GM president Smith.

They maintained that Moore had pirated their research (Moore had worked briefly for Nader and thus was privy to the ideas of the people working with Nader's organization). Nader put a price on this supposed abuse, demanding $30,000 from Moore as compensation for the financial and material support his organization had provided for *Roger & Me* and other projects.[45]

These animated debates provoked by *Roger & Me*'s hard-hitting arguments served as a preview of later public disputes surrounding Moore's subsequent books, television programs, and films. Books such as *Adventures in a TV Nation, Downsize This! Stupid White Men . . . and Other Sorry Excuses for the State of the Nation!* and *Dude, Where's My Country?* became best sellers and highly controversial because of their opinionated approach to sensitive political issues. Moore's 1997 movie *The Big One* questioned the practices of America's large corporations but attracted only limited curiosity and interest among the public and the critics. *Bowling for Columbine*, his 2002 film about the nation's culture of violence and its love affair with the gun, resonated to a much greater degree. It attracted huge audiences and aroused heated discussions about the United States' comparatively high homicide rate and the role of firearms in American society, and it won the Academy Award for best documentary. By the time Moore was promoting *Bowling for Columbine*, a U.S.-led war with Iraq seemed likely. U.S. foreign policy was increasingly on the filmmaker's mind, and Moore sometimes associated *Columbine*'s message about domestic violence with his concern about violence in foreign policy. When describing the message of *Bowling for Columbine* for *Time* magazine in October 2002, Moore explained, "It's a film about why we're so violent toward each other, and why we tend to export a lot of this violence around the world."[46]

Michael Moore may have drawn some inspiration, too, from his only "Hollywood"-style fiction film, *Canadian Bacon* (1995). That comedy with a serious twist is about a president with falling popularity ratings who decides that tough talk about going to war against a weak foreign nation could help boost his appeal with the voters. The president chooses Canada as the supposedly troublesome enemy, and the character played by John Candy, a gun-toting private militia type, goes overboard, stimulated by the silly anti-Canada rhetoric. Moore told the press that his original idea for the movie had emerged back in the early 1990s, during U.S. participation in the Persian Gulf War. He had been amazed at how easily a president could whip up war sentiment against a country that had not previously been seen as an archenemy. *Canadian Bacon* mixed an antiwar message with humor, but it failed to obtain the financial backing (for distribution and advertising) that Moore sought. Furthermore, John Candy died before the movie's release in American theaters, and a comedy featuring a dead star seemed problematic. The movie did not draw much of an audience, and another Hollywood film with a related theme, *Wag the Dog*, attracted much more public interest.

By early 2003, Michael Moore sensed that a real president was about to take his nation into a real war against a questionable enemy. The seemingly invented danger in this case came not from Canada but from Iraq. Leaders in the Bush administration appeared determined to depose Saddam Hussein through an invasion and occupation led by U.S. forces. This issue was more sharply focused than any subject Moore had previously addressed. *Fahrenheit 9/11* had greater potential to excite public discussion than his earlier movies had, because it attacked more definable targets. In previous films, Moore had gone after vague problems such as downsizing in a manufacturing industry and the culture of violence in the United States. His new target was more delineated, familiar, and current: it was the Bush administration's attempt to connect in the public mind the 9/11 attacks and the activities of Saddam Hussein. This subject seemed especially inviting because Moore could introduce his hard-hitting critique during an election year, when he might influence voters and even affect the outcome of the presidential contest.

The situation was naturally volatile. Michael Moore, a strongly committed filmmaker, discovered an ideal topic to serve his populist agenda. He intended to make a stinging yet entertaining film that would excite lively debates about the war and the presidency in the United States and abroad. After years of experience as a magazine editor, book author, television producer, and moviemaker, Moore was now well equipped to turn his new production into a political event.

2 The Anatomy of
Fahrenheit 9/11

Since no American-made documentary in modern times has received more scrutiny for its treatment of specific political subjects or more criticism for its style of presentation, it is worthwhile to examine the structure of *Fahrenheit 9/11* and its handling of historical details. This chapter deals with the strategies Michael Moore employed to make his political case. It discusses Moore's tactics in attacking the national news media and singling out the president as a principal target in the film. This chapter also explores the comic approaches Moore used in *Fahrenheit 9/11* and points out that he had developed these strategies in earlier productions. Finally, the discussion draws attention to the importance of "primary sources" in constructing Moore's political critique.

Criticism of the news media was central to the thesis of *Fahrenheit 9/11*. That is why Moore tweaked the title of Ray Bradbury's famous sci-fi novel, *Fahrenheit 451*, when naming his movie. Bradbury's reference was to the temperature needed to burn books in a subtly oppressive society. In that future world, citizens lived in comfort, believing what their leaders told them to think. Moore's movie title suggested that the message in Bradbury's tale was relevant. Journalism had failed the American people. Instead of awakening citizens to the administration's lies, the press extended the broadcast range of those misrepresentations. "I refuse to participate in the brainwashing that the media were doing to the American public," Moore asserted.[1]

Like many artists who interpret issues through film, Michael Moore simplified and dramatized his story. He examined a broad subject but made it appear more tightly focused by establishing a principal target for his narrative. President George W. Bush served as that convenient fall guy. *Fahrenheit 9/11* personalized Moore's criticism of national policies by making the president the "heavy" in the narrative (and the object of many of its jokes). The movie's personal attack on the nation's leader greatly irritated defenders of the president, but Moore's strategy was a familiar technique in the filmmaking profession. It is practiced often in documentary production and especially in fictional feature films from Hollywood that deal with real-life figures from history and politics. One individual often serves as the symbolic villain in the presentation. There are, of course, many other figures who are to blame for the historical problems under consideration in these movies. But audiences can easily become confused if films diffuse responsibility and attribute culpability to many factors and numerous perpetrators. Establishing a single culprit excites interest, clarifies issues, and makes a multifaceted examination of events more understandable.

If Michael Moore had been writing a scholarly book about the Bush administration's questionable handling of foreign policy after the 9/11 crisis, he would have had to give detailed attention to the role of the several important people who helped shape policies. Vice President Dick Cheney would deserve many pages of discussion, as would other prominent leaders in Washington at the time, such as Donald Rumsfeld, Colin Powell, Condoleezza Rice, and Paul Wolfowitz. There would be attention, as well, to individuals who were less familiar to the American public, such as Douglas Feith, the undersecretary of defense for security policy, and Lewis "Scooter" Libby, Vice President Cheney's chief of staff. Although this complex coverage would be essential in a major publication, it would undermine the success of a documentary production. Filmmakers understand that they must give a movie's principal "problem" a distinct personality. One individual's behavior serves to represent in broad ways the activities of the many. Other leading players in the cinematic history can make brief appearances, but their involvement in events is often treated symbolically rather than methodically.

Evidence of this dramatic strategy appears throughout *Fahrenheit 9/11*. In every segment, George W. Bush is the principal target of criticism. He is the villain who, supposedly, escaped full service in the National Guard as a young man, benefited from suspicious business deals as an entrepreneur, enjoyed ties with the Saudi royal family, failed to heed intelligence warnings about a possible al Qaeda attack, and manipulated public opinion when driving his nation toward war with Iraq. Major figures in his administration make only cameo appearances in *Fahrenheit 9/11*, and their on-screen moments are typically comic. In one scene, Attorney General John Ashcroft sings an original patriotic ditty; in another, Deputy Secretary of Defense Paul Wolfowitz carefully combs his hair in preparation for an on-camera appearance. These symbolic elements support one of Moore's principal points: that the people who designed President Bush's controversial national policies were not truly individuals of extraordinary mental and moral stature. By showing these people in nonscripted moments and awkward situations, Moore hints that the leaders in Washington are human beings like the rest of us. They, too, can have clay feet. Furthermore, these clips display national leaders in various states of cosmetic preparation for appearances on television. Through these images, Moore suggests that their policies as well as their faces were made up to impress the public. Americans were not viewing reality when they watched those leaders on television. The faces they saw and policies they heard about were cosmetically enhanced.[2]

Fahrenheit 9/11's enemies not only failed to recognize the traditions of simplification and dramatization in filmmaking when hurling verbal stones against it; they also failed to acknowledge that comedy has become an accepted standard for communicating political ideas in the mass media. Political satire with a serious bite has been gaining substantial popularity in recent decades. The Daily Show's appeal among young Americans represented a stunning example of that attraction in the year of Fahrenheit 9/11's release. Jon Stewart's comic but biting news reporting became a popular sensation.

There were many examples of comedy with a political sting throughout the U.S. entertainment media in 2004. On the Left, the caustic and provocative comedian Bill Maher delivered political zingers on his HBO program and in numerous appearances on TV talk shows. Comedian Dennis Miller offered humorous discussions of social and political topics with a conservative orientation on CNBC. Radio carried the nation's preeminent right-wing talk master, Rush Limbaugh, who entertained audiences daily with a blend of anger, wit, and humor. Al Franken, a familiar jokester on the Left, maintained a busy schedule as an anti-Bush satirist in 2004, and he was instrumental in launching a liberal talk-radio station that mixed humor with political criticism. Joe Scarborough, who hosted his own show on MSNBC, delighted right-oriented viewers with amusing slights against liberals and Democrats. It had become clear by 2004 that many Americans enjoyed listening to political discussions that made them laugh as well as think.

While critics lambasted Michael Moore for examining political subjects superficially, playing for laughs rather than insights, the filmmaker defended his technique as useful for effective communication. Humor, he claimed, was essential for attracting the attention of audiences. Unfortunately, said Moore, many Americans with his point of view did not draw laughs when making their case. "If more people on the left would redis-cover their sense of humor, they would be more successful," Moore coun-seled.[3] Anger alone would not suffice to awaken the public, he maintained. American voters who were still undecided about the upcoming presidential election were not likely to respond positively to a long, unrelenting cin-ematic assault on President Bush, even if the criticisms raised in the film were valid. Audiences do not wish to listen to that kind of diatribe, Moore argued. "Nobody wants to be around it," he said. "I don't want to be around it. If you told me this movie, 'Fahrenheit 9/11,' it's just an anti-Bush movie, I don't know if I would go to see it. . . . Why would I waste two hours in the theater to learn that Bush is bad if I already felt that way?"[4]

Michael Moore's comic style, fine-tuned over the course of years spent writing books and articles, producing films, and creating television shows, takes seven forms. Together, these comic approaches represent a Moore trademark. They are easily recognized as his storytelling strategy, just as the Ken Burns style has been influential in documentary filmmaking. Moore's technique, like Burns's, has inspired imitators. For example, in the year of *Fahrenheit 9/11*'s release, Morgan Spurlock brought out a humorous filmic assault on the fat-building properties of food sold at McDonald's. In his entertaining documentary *Super-Size Me*, Spurlock copied the personal and comedic style Moore had pioneered in *Roger & Me* and other films.

Fahrenheit 9/11 introduced a broad array of comic techniques designed to make audiences laugh and think. Following are the seven principal charac-teristics of Moore's humorous genre.

1. *The Comic Investigator.* Moore is, himself, a humorous presence in these films, and he openly advertised this strategy through the title of his first popular documentary, *Roger & Me.* The filmmaker's large physical frame draws smiles, and his casual clothing and baseball-style cap signal a playful attitude. Moore's proletarian garb also suggests sympathy for the common people rather than the country's wealthy and powerful citizens. An absence of formal dress in diverse social and political situations suggests, too, an attitude of irreverence. Moore's untidy appearance hints that he will not be swayed by pretensions and will not suffer fools gladly.

As several movie reviewers observed, Moore's physical presence in *Fahrenheit 9/11* was not as strong as it had been in his previous documen-taries. He occasionally came into a frame in *Fahrenheit 9/11*, and he served as the story's narrator, but Moore spent surprisingly little time in front of the camera. Miramax's Harvey Weinstein, who played an important role in getting the film distributed when Michael Eisner's Disney chose not to handle the movie, was initially concerned about this tactic. "You're the star they're coming to see," he told Moore, urging him to step into the picture in a number of scenes. Moore felt, however, that this story called for a more serious reportorial design than in his previous films. The moviemaker's presence throughout the story could complicate the effort to deliver hard-hitting messages. This film "doesn't need me running around with my exclamation points," he said.[5] Moore also recognized that making the president the butt of jokes would better support his thesis about failed leadership than would trying to turn his own activities into the principal source of humor and thought. Accordingly, Moore informed the press that he had given the best laughs to George W. Bush.

2. *Juxtaposition of Comic and Serious Elements.* Moore understands the value of placing serious and humorous material side by side. This practice surprises and amuses audiences and helps accentuate political messages. In *Fahrenheit 9/11*, Moore employed the technique by overlaying images of political activities with suggestive music. For example, a segment about the U.S. government's failure to capture Osama bin Laden after the 9/11 tragedy featured the song "Gotta Get Outta Here." Moore's report on Bush's failure to appear for a physical when he was in the Air National Guard was supported with J. J. Cale's song "Cocaine," and the Go-Gos' "Vacation" accompanied a report about President Bush's many recreational visits to his Texas ranch. REM's "Shining Happy People" played over pictures of the Bush family and their business associates. Trick photography was also used to draw laughs and make references to old cultural icons. At one point, George W. Bush was shown in cowboy attire, and then an imitation of *Bonanza*'s opening credits placed the president's face where Lorne Greene's would be. Later, when reporting on the U.S. government's failure to interview Saudis about their knowledge of Osama bin Laden, the film showed Sergeant Joe Friday (Jack Webb) of *Dragnet* looking for the facts. Through this juxtaposition, Moore made the serious point that representatives of the U.S. government should have presented tough questions to the Saudi nationals who managed to fly out of the United States shortly after September 11, 2001.

3. *The Ambush.* Michael Moore has become famous for surprising individuals who are unprepared to deal with his penetrating and irritating questions. This approach was central to *Roger & Me*, since the entire film was about Moore's humorous attempts to obtain an interview with General Motors chairman Roger Smith. Another notable ambush occurred in *The Big*

One when Moore interviewed Philip Knight, the founder and head of Nike Corporation. Knight was expecting to give Moore an impressive report on his corporation's good deeds, but instead, the filmmaker asked unsettling questions about Nike's tendency to farm out production to factories in Southeast Asia, where subcontractors paid workers poorly and required them to work under difficult conditions. *Bowling for Columbine* featured a visit to the estate of actor and National Rifle Association spokesman Charlton Heston. Heston was clearly caught off guard and in a state of naiveté, for he invited Moore into his home. After some pleasantries, Moore battered the aging actor with penetrating questions about his defense of gun ownership, and Heston began to look trapped and confused. In *Fahrenheit 9/11* Moore practiced the technique by appearing in Washington, D.C., where he asked various congressmen if they wished to send their children to Iraq to serve in the U.S. armed forces. Most of the legislators waved him off and appeared eager to escape the eye of his camera. One individual responded to some of Moore's questions, but the politician's nervously delivered comments appeared to undermine his arguments rather than enhance them.

Moore's familiar ambush tactics often get laughs and help accentuate his points, but they also arouse considerable controversy. Critics have argued that these ambushes are unfair, and sometimes this is evident to viewers as well. In *The Big One*, for instance, despite Moore's efforts to trick and embarrass the Nike CEO, audiences can see that Knight is a well-meaning executive who seems more enlightened than the typical U.S. corporate leader. The interview with Charlton Heston in *Bowling for Columbine* seems inappropriate, too, since news of Heston's diagnosis with Alzheimer's disease had reached the press by the time Moore's film hit the theaters. Critics also point out that Moore does not represent his purposes honestly when he seeks these interviews, and he manipulates the evidence by editing the material, including only that which supports his case and creates the greatest embarrassment for the interviewee. This complaint was certainly relevant to the debates about *Fahrenheit 9/11*, for detractors argued that the congressman who spoke to Moore made some important statements that did not appear in the film. In short, ambushes are fundamental elements of the Moore strategy, and they are also among the most controversial components.

4. *The Antic.* Michael Moore frequently stages humorous events for laughs, but also to make a serious point. This technique draws attention to the basic problem under study. One stunt performed years ago involved criticism of the Philip Morris tobacco company: Moore gathered a group

of tracheotomy patients at the corporation's headquarters to sing Christ-mas carols through their voice boxes. One of the most memorable stunts in *Fahrenheit 9/11* featured Moore driving around the Capitol in an ice cream truck, reading the Patriot Act over the loudspeaker. The filmmaker reported that most members of Congress who had hurriedly voted for the act after the 9/11 disaster had not actually read its many provisions. He aimed to edu-cate them. This antic drew laughs, but it also hammered an important point that the filmmaker wanted to make.

5. *The Outtake. Fahrenheit 9/11* turned this politically charged but humor-ous technique into a major strategy for challenging the reputation of Presi-dent Bush and leaders in his administration. Outtakes are sections of video or film that do not appear in the final, edited version. In television produc-tions, for instance, some outtakes represent material that was intended for broadcast but did not turn out as planned. TV programs occasionally feature compilations of such footage for laughs, showing actors flubbing their lines and chuckling at their mistakes. Other outtakes, such as the ones Michael Moore incorporated in *Fahrenheit 9/11*, come from the minutes shortly before a broadcast is set to begin. In those moments, interviewees may make faces or attend to their personal needs, confidently expecting that their actions will never appear on television or movie screens.

Some of the most pertinent examples of outtakes in *Fahrenheit 9/11* per-tained to the behavior of President George W. Bush. Three stand out, and each received much discussion in the national media (these are addressed in a subsequent chapter). In a particularly damning segment, Moore showed the president looking devious and childish shortly before addressing the nation on television to explain his reasons for leading the United States into a war with Iraq. A second much-discussed moment in the film showed the president on the golf course, speaking briefly with reporters. "We must stop the terror," said the chief executive. "I call upon all nations to do everything they can to stop these terrorist killers. Thank you. Now watch this drive." Bush then slammed a golf ball off the tee. A third and especially provocative outtake involved the president's appearance at a Sarasota, Florida, elemen-tary school. The film showed him reading a book to the youngsters when special assistant Andrew Card appeared and whispered a message into the president's ear: "Sir, America is under attack." Time-lapse photography in-dicated that the president did not leave the room for nearly seven minutes after receiving the disturbing news.

How did Michael Moore obtain such video material, which had not been seen before by many Americans? One would think that such potentially embarrassing imagery would be kept under wraps to prevent filmmakers such as Moore from getting their hands on it. Surprisingly, Moore and his researchers had little difficulty securing the unflattering and memorable imagery. Video coverage was available through television satellite feeds, which are typically edited by producers at individual television stations. The most surprising and embarrassing video evidence, showing seven minutes of inaction after the president was informed of the attacks of 9/11, fell into Moore's hands with little effort. His research team called the Sarasota school to ask if anyone had made a recording of the president's visit. Sure enough, a teacher had set up a video camera to capture the important moment in the school's history. School officials were happy to turn over their coverage of the entire event, as long as Moore's organization would pay for a copy of the videotape. Through such a small and inexpensive effort, Moore and his team secured one of *Fahrenheit 9/11*'s most damning images of the president.[6]

6. *Guerrilla Theater.* Moore's comic approach includes brief satirical sketches that lampoon national programs and policies presented to the public as serious matters. This technique serves to expose the ridiculousness of some official claims. One of *Fahrenheit 9/11*'s most effective exercises in guerrilla theater related to the Bush administration's promotion of a "Coalition of the Willing"—those nations that were joining and supporting the U.S.-led war in Iraq. The administration insisted that the United States was not acting alone in Iraq; supposedly, many other nations were partners in joint operations to bring freedom, peace, and democracy to the Iraqis. From Moore's perspective, the United States and Great Britain carried the bulk of responsibilities in these actions. Other nations had been enticed to participate in the coalition primarily to give the war and the occupation the appearance of a broad-based international effort. Moore enjoyed making fun of the minor countries in the coalition and their weak and generally insignificant contributions. His "roll call" for the Bush administration's "Coalition of the Willing" featured a narrator with a deep voice suggesting that the Republic of Costa Rica and Iceland, nations without armies, were ready for action. A reference to Romania's contribution to the coalition included a scene from a Dracula movie. The narrator's mention of the Netherlands' participation showed individuals indulging in drugs, and a reference to

Afghanistan's contribution featured poppies growing in a field (suggesting that nation's role as an international source for cocaine).

7. *The Amusing Yet Revealing Quote.* Michael Moore often includes interview material that is likely to amaze audiences, make them laugh, and illustrate a major point in his thesis. These brief segments, sometimes consisting of only one or two sentences, offer surprising and revealing perspectives on events. For instance, *Fahrenheit 9/11* featured a brief discussion with U.S. Representative John Conyers Jr., who observed that his fellow congressmen had passed the Patriot Act in quick order and did not have an opportunity to read its many complex and controversial provisions. When Moore feigned shock, Conyers replied, "Sit down, my son. We don't read most of the bills. Do you really know what that would entail if we were to read every bill that we pass?" This interesting revelation amazed many viewers, who believed that their elected representatives gave careful consideration to the terms of each piece of proposed legislation. Another memorable segment featured pop music artist Britney Spears urging support for President Bush's policies. Chewing gum in a manner that suggested an unsophisticated perspective on politics (and life), Spears said, "Honestly, I think we should just trust our president in every decision that he makes and we should support that, you know, and, uh, be faithful in what happens." Audiences could chuckle at the young artist's naiveté yet recognize that many people had expressed similar sentiments. They were inclined to express unquestioning loyalty to the president and his policies.

Some of the amusing quotes in *Fahrenheit 9/11* showed President Bush making statements that he intended to be serious. The president's awkward use of the English language invoked laughs in these instances, yet the movie's focus on Bush's struggles with syntax also drew attention to important political issues. For instance, *Fahrenheit 9/11* depicted the president attempting to explain why the Iraqis were putting up such strong resistance against U.S. forces. "I wouldn't be happy if I were occupied either," the president commented. This ungraceful statement amused audiences, yet its employment in the film nicely served the filmmaker's purposes. One of Moore's principal points in the movie was that many Iraqis, like most nationals around the world, naturally resisted the presence of a large foreign army and bureaucracy in their country. They viewed Americans in Iraq as occupiers. In the movie's final scene, the president was shown struggling to articulate an old saying and jumbling the words. "There's an old saying in Tennessee, I know it's in Texas, probably in Tennessee," he said. "Fool me once, shame on . . . shame on you. . . . Fool me, you can't get fooled again." Knowing that laughter surely filled the theater after this quote, Moore reminded audiences of his message indirectly, saying, "For once, we agreed."

Of course, *Fahrenheit 9/11* communicated important political messages in serious ways as well as humorous ones, and Moore employed primary sources to make many of these serious points. The term *primary sources* implies the use of original materials discovered through careful research. When evaluating scholarship, for instance, historians often applaud an investigator who uncovers distinctive new evidence that had not been featured in previous studies. An article or a book contributes notably to "new knowledge," say scholars, when it does not depend on merely a reinterpretation of evidence that has already been widely circulated. Impressive research incorporates original information that has not previously received serious public consideration.

Fahrenheit 9/11 did not feature a broad array of evidence *never* seen before, but Michael Moore and his production team deserve credit for uncovering numerous primary film and video sources that had received relatively little attention in the mainstream national media prior to the movie's release. Archival researchers working on *Fahrenheit 9/11* uncovered a rich variety of intriguing evidence that was generally unfamiliar to the American public during the summer of 2004. Moore's camera operators also managed to film some intriguing scenes on their own. Each of these primary sources in *Fahrenheit 9/11*, standing independently, is distinctive but not necessarily extraordinary, since some television-based journalists offered related news stories and pictures. The large aggregate of original source material featured in the movie, however, constitutes a significant accomplishment and a useful contribution to the public discourse on politics. Moore enhanced the quality of that dialogue by exposing audiences to many images and words that were not available in typical television news reporting during the summer of 2004.

Before exploring these elements, it is useful to note that Moore gave some familiar source materials particularly memorable treatment in *Fahrenheit 9/11* by handling them in unconventional ways. One of the most impressive examples in this regard was his portrayal of the destruction of the World Trade Center in New York City. Instead of reproducing images that were already quite familiar to the public, Moore showed a black screen supported by sounds from the tragedy. Then he showed the faces of shocked New Yorkers and debris from the burning buildings. This imaginative treatment of familiar visual evidence encouraged audiences to think about the artist's purpose in presenting the disturbing material in this fashion. That brief segment demonstrated Moore's greater skill and aesthetic sophistication, since such artistic touches had been less evident in Moore's earlier productions.

Some of the most controversial primary evidence in the film pertains to the thoughts, behavior, and experiences of people in the U.S. armed services. It is extraordinary that Moore could make this treatment seem shocking and disturbing to American audiences, since TV viewers in the United States had been exposed to many hours of coverage regarding military operations in Iraq. Yet, as Moore's film suggested, much of that media attention in the fist months of reporting had been filtered. Television coverage of soldiers' activities had been limited mostly to information that put the servicemen and their actions in favorable light. "Embedded" journalists described the soldiers' quick progress in the war and their success in liberating Iraq from the evil dictator Saddam Hussein. Television showed attempts by army and marine units to clear cities of insurgents in the Sunni triangle. It also showed U.S. soldiers trying to bring electricity and water to the Iraqi people, build schools for them, and train the Iraqis to participate in democratic elections. This media coverage tended to accent feel-good stories, and in the first months of reporting, there was relatively little attention given to disturbing news about the experiences of men and women in the U.S. armed forces in Iraq.

Michael Moore was correct when he argued that the mass media provided a service for the Bush administration by broadcasting these rosy news stories. In fact, television news organizations gave substantial broadcast time to various cheerleaders for the administration's policies when the information coming out of Iraq began to look troubling. As the insurgency grew and terrorist acts increased substantially, various Republican politicians and conservative pundits appeared on television in 2003 and 2004 to lambaste the media for negativism. These critics charged that network and cable news coverage of conditions in Iraq imitated a strategy evident in television's reporting of local events in the United States. As the saying goes in the news business, if it bleeds, it leads. Sounding very much like Vice President Spiro Agnew, who had criticized the media for its supposedly depressing stories about the Vietnam War during the Nixon administration, modern-day Republicans and conservatives blasted the network and cable media for giving too much attention to dark news from Iraq.

Bush supporters asked: where are the important, upbeat stories about favorable developments in Iraq? U.S. civilians and soldiers were making significant progress, they insisted. Thousands of children were now attending school and getting immunizations. Women were finding new opportunities to pursue education and plan careers—choices that had been less available to them during Saddam Hussein's rule. Preparations were under way to bring democratic practices to a people that had experienced only dictatorship. These were uplifting and truthful stories about impressive developments in Iraq, said the champions of the Bush administration's policies. The liberal media were giving Americans at home the wrong impression about conditions in Iraq by privileging reports about shootings and explosions. There were some isolated incidents, the critics confessed, but these troublesome activities did not represent the larger picture of progress. Overall, the U.S. government's program of liberation and assistance appeared to be succeeding.

As the difficulties of Americans and other foreigners in Iraq increased in 2003 and 2004, the American news media did indeed expand their coverage, but network and cable producers tended to broadcast images that were quite different from the ones Michael Moore projected in *Fahrenheit 9/11*. Moore presented a counternarrative and a counterpicture portfolio of the war and its impact on U.S. servicemen. The words and pictures featured in *Fahrenheit 9/11* were not pretty, but that ugliness is what made them distinctive. While the mainstream news media tended to limit their coverage to attacks led by Iraqi soldiers and insurgents, focusing on the destruction of U.S. military equipment and the casualties suffered by U.S. forces, *Fahrenheit 9/11* explored the war's psychological impact on U.S. servicemen. Moore's film moved beyond the familiar images of burned-out vehicles and injured American soldiers, and it went beyond the well-covered stories of U.S. military officers planning to reply to the enemy's attacks with new sweeps and security checks. Moore looked at the troubled souls of the soldiers and marines, and his treatment of this subject aroused considerable controversy.

In this segment of the film, Moore explained that unfortunate behavior can occur when the nation sends good young Americans on a bad mission. He suggested that the controversial actions of some servicemen were really the fault of the nation's leaders who had sent the soldiers to Iraq. When placed in a dangerous situation in which they are viewed as enemy invaders, some young men in U.S. military uniforms are likely to be insensitive to human rights—in fact, insensitive to the basic humanity of the Iraqi people, whether friend or foe.

Three segments of *Fahrenheit 9/11* communicated this thesis with particular force. One scene showed a U.S. soldier attached to an armored vehicle reporting that he and his buddies listened to hard rock music to pump up their enthusiasm for combat, killing, and destruction. They could hook up songs to the sound system of their tank and get an "ultimate rush," the soldier explained. A song's lyrics proclaimed, "The roof is on fire," and a singer exclaimed, "Burn, motherf—, burn." In another segment, a cameraman followed U.S. troops as they made a Christmas Eve raid on a home. The sounds of "Silent Night" and images of Santa Claus provided a surreal backdrop for the actions that followed. American soldiers burst into a home, found the young man they were searching for, and prepared to take him away. His distraught mother claimed that he was only a college student and had done nothing wrong. Such video coverage can excite the movie audience's memories of past Hollywood movies featuring Nazi authorities breaking into homes and seizing innocent citizens in front of their frightened and desperate families. This image was certainly familiar to viewers who had seen Steven Spielberg's *Schindler's List*. Finally, Moore's film depicted the harassment of Iraqi prisoners by American soldiers. Several servicemen were shown surrounding an Iraqi man covered with a blanket. The prisoner evidently had an erection, and the Americans taunted him in a scene suggestive of the sexual, psychological, and physical abuse that later came to light in connection with the Abu Ghraib prison in Iraq. Moore's critics pointed to these upsetting images when they blasted his film for misrepresenting the American experience in Iraq.

Although *Fahrenheit 9/11* showed that some soldiers abused the tremendous authority they had over the lives of individual Iraqis, it also demonstrated that other servicemen became physical and psychological victims of the insurgency and the U.S. military actions in Iraq. Moore took audiences where the Bush administration and the mainstream media tended not to go. While the administration worked strenuously to keep images of body bags and coffins off the TV screen (they were not good for morale at home or abroad), Moore showed, however briefly, a number of caskets. Television reporting revealed little of the suffering experienced by injured veterans. *Fahrenheit 9/11* took audiences to Walter Reed Hospital and to Blanchfield Army Community Hospital at Fort Campbell, Kentucky, where many young

Americans who had been badly wounded by the explosions and the bullets were being treated. Some soldiers had lost limbs, others suffered from nerve damage, and some appeared to be deeply scarred emotionally as well as physically. Additionally, Moore's film introduced audiences to soldiers who sounded dubious about the war. "It's not that easy to conquer a country, is it?" asks one obviously frustrated young American in Iraq. Another says, "I don't have any clue as to why we're here. If [Secretary of Defense] Donald Rumsfeld were here, I'd ask for his resignation." A third soldier, commenting back in the United States, boldly claimed that he would not go back to Iraq if recalled for service there. The young African American, standing in full uniform, told Moore that he did not want to kill people in Iraq who had not done anything to harm him.

The most memorable criticism of the war in *Fahrenheit 9/11* came from Lila Lipscomb, a native of California who had lived in Flint, Michigan, since 1985. Her commentary was startling and impressive because it was so unlike the typical reports about servicemen's families that are featured in the "human-interest" segment of television news programs. In most of those reports, the parents of young servicemen and -women in Iraq are depicted as steely American citizens who eagerly recite patriotic platitudes. The injury or death of a son or daughter does not seem to shake their fundamental support of President Bush and his policies. These parents who have experienced a personal tragedy do not question the president's rationale for the military attack on Iraq and the subsequent occupation—at least not while a camera is directed at them.

During the final twenty minutes of *Fahrenheit 9/11*, however, Michael Moore cleverly presents a counterperspective through his interview with a super-patriotic woman who identifies herself as a "conservative Democrat." Lila Lipscomb has been flying the American flag outside her home for years, but she is also willing to question actions that appear to dishonor the ideals she associates with that flag. Lipscomb is a perfect source for the expression of discontent about the war in Iraq. She is from a gung-ho military family. Four of her five brothers served in the military, three of them in Vietnam. Her elder daughters served during the Gulf War, and a nephew recently signed up for military service. Lipscomb has advised her relatives and other young men to join the military, not only for patriotic reasons but also because good jobs are difficult to find in depressed Flint. The armed forces provide a way out, an opportunity to obtain technical training and improved career options.

Moore shows Lipscomb in emotion-filled moments near the end of the movie to hammer his thesis about the war's impact on American families. He films Lipscomb while she reads one of the last letters she received from her son, Michael Pederson. In a particularly telling statement, the young sergeant expresses doubts about the mission planned by authorities in Washington, D.C. "He got us out here for nothing whatsoever," Michael says of President Bush's decision. Lipscomb tells Moore that her son died when his Black Hawk helicopter was shot down by enemy fire in Iraq. Later, Lipscomb goes to Washington, and looks at the White House. "I finally have a place to put all of my pain and anger," she tells Moore.

Another memorable primary source in Moore's movie involves the way young men are recruited for military service. In that segment of the film, Moore plays the class card. He argues that recruiters find the streets and parking lots of poor communities, such as those in Flint, Michigan, much more attractive hunting grounds for potential volunteers than locations in affluent neighborhoods. As Lila Lipscomb maintains, the young people in Flint have meager job prospects, but by joining the army, marines, navy, or air force, they can escape that economic devastation. Surprisingly, Moore encountered no resistance when he tried to accompany the marine recruiters as they made their rounds. He just hooked up microphones to their bodies and filmed their efforts.

Fahrenheit 9/11 reveals that these hunters for volunteers actively engage potential clients, give out business cards, and speak excitedly about the attractions of the armed services. They sound like salesmen who might accost browsers in a car lot and give them a hard-sell pitch to buy an automobile. Nothing seems to block the recruiters' determined efforts to win over potential soldiers. "I've got a wife and kid now," a young prospect tells the two marines. "Even more reason to join," one of them replies confidently.

Some of the notable primary sources that Michael Moore incorporated into his movie related not to military intervention in a foreign country but to political problems back in the United States. One of the domestic stories that excited strong audience interest was Moore's report early in the movie about the failed efforts of several African American representatives in Congress to get a single senator to endorse their challenge to the presidential election results of 2000. Fahrenheit 9/11 shows Vice President Al Gore presiding over his own defeat. As head of the Senate, he declares that protests by legislators are unacceptable under the rules of the assembly, since no member of the Senate has formally supported their case. This event received only slight attention in the national media at the time it oc-curred, and most Americans were unaware of it. Placing this intriguing pri-mary source near the beginning of the movie was a surprising strategy that Moore would maintain throughout the film. He often presented words and images that seemed to be generally unfamiliar to the viewers. The material seemed fresh, surprising, and sometimes alarming. It gave *Fahrenheit 9/11* a distinctive quality, signaling that Moore intended to examine and exhibit the unique, not just the familiar.

The film's segment about the failed effort to challenge the 2000 election in the Senate evidently made an impact four years later. Democratic sena-tor Barbara Boxer, affected by the emotion-laden coverage of the Senate's handling of the 2000 presidential election results, agreed to back a related challenge in 2005. This action, dubbed "Boxer's Rebellion," drew sena-tors into nearly four hours of contentious debate in January 2005. On the night of January 7, 2005, television programs carried lively commentary on Senator Boxer's actions and the significance of the Senate's dismissal of election challenges four years before. Chris Matthews, Bill O'Reilly, Paul Begala, Robert Novak, and the staff on PBS's *Washington Week* offered sharp views on Moore's message and Boxer's actions. And Michael Moore con-tributed to those discussions through an appearance that evening on Jay Leno's show.

Just about every section of *Fahrenheit 9/11* became grist for the political mills in 2004. Defenders of President Bush's policies angrily dissected and analyzed each major section of the movie and judged the production false and misleading. They lambasted its creator as an irresponsible agitator. Moore, they said, manipulated and distorted evidence to promote his radi-cally partisan agenda. His movie presented an extreme, radical perspective. It is useful, next, to examine these charges in detail.

3 A Sinister Exercise

Fahrenheit 9/11 raised big questions about President George W. Bush's domestic and foreign policies, yet angry responses to the movie made by pundits and politicians on the Right, as well as some objectors from the print and electronic media, gave relatively little attention to those important queries. The film's detractors concentrated their attack, instead, on the filmmaker and some of his smaller political arguments. They treated Michael Moore's character as a major issue in these debates and attempted to make some of the film's minor points the main subjects of contention. These critics essentially conceded Moore's principal arguments by default, since they did not engage them in a sustained and detailed manner. Nevertheless, their criticisms attracted a good deal of attention in the public arena. Eventually, their complaints about the movie helped the cause of conservatives, Republicans, and defenders of the president's policies. Many Americans who encountered these negative responses, including millions who had not seen the movie, sensed that *Fahrenheit 9/11* was a problematic work of art.

Often rhetoric served to bolster the Right's principal case against *Fahrenheit 9/11*. Conservatives who disagreed with (or despised) Moore's politics blasted the movie in contemptuous language but provided few specifics as to the source of their emotional salvos. The main thrust of their critique involved damning language rather than damaging evidence. White House communications director Dan Bartlett offered one notably harsh dismissal. "It's so outrageously false, it's not even worth a comment," declared Bartlett.[1] The White House spokesman said, "If I wanted to see a good fiction movie, I might go to see *Shrek* or something, but I doubt I'll be seeing *Fahrenheit 9/11*." Others on the Right brushed off Moore's film with similarly contemptuous language. Republican strategist Jack Burkman exclaimed on MSNBC's *Scarborough Country*, "The whole thing is filled with nothing but lies." He argued that the movie represented "one big cycle of fraud and distorted images." Stalinists and Nazis worked in a manner similar to Michael Moore, Burkman asserted, "not in terms of scope and magnitude, but in terms of perception." James Bowman, writing for the conservative publication *New Criterion*, claimed that the movie was filled with "innuendo and malicious suggestion."[2] Writing in the conservative magazine *National Review*, Jonah Goldberg described the film as "a wonderful lie."[3] A commentary in another right-oriented publication, *American Spectator*, dismissed the film as "unscrupulous, unnuanced, unmitigated propaganda laced with buffoonery."[4] Siobahn Guiney of the conservative organization Move America Forward declared that *Fahrenheit 9/11* was "a military-bashing piece of propaganda."[5] Guiney's organization characterized the movie as "a collection of lies which leads to a big lie." It blasted *Fahrenheit 9/11* as a training film for al Qaeda and a defense brief for Saddam Hussein (who was awaiting trial after his capture).[6]

Critics on the Right also directed verbal attacks against the man who made the movie. "Michael Moore Hates America," declared the title of Mike Wilson's anti-Moore documentary. David T. Hardy and Jason Clarke communicated their view of Moore and his work through the title of a book: *Michael Moore Is a Big Fat Stupid White Man*. They accused the filmmaker of "serial mendacity."[7] Conservative stalwart William F. Buckley dismissed Moore as a "comic ideologue," while radio and television talk-show host Bill O'Reilly compared Moore to the Nazi propaganda minister Joseph Goebbels. Not surprisingly, George H. W. Bush, the former president and father of George W., joined these expressions of contempt. The elder Bush called Moore a "slimeball" for engaging in "a vicious attack on our son."[8]

Citizens and journalists complained that Moore exploited the common people he featured in his movies in order to draw large audiences and advance his career. Californian Chris Piombo, in a letter to the editor of the *Sacramento Bee*, accused Moore of trying to make money "from the pain and suffering of others," including unemployed autoworkers, the victims of Columbine, and brave American soldiers in Iraq.[9] Mark Steyn, a conservative writing for *Spectator*, described the movie as a "Bush-bashing tract" and said that Moore dwelled on the grief of the bereaved mother from Flint, Michigan, "at exploitative length."[10] Mark Kermode, commenting for the *Observer*, took a similar position, calling the film's treatment of Lila Lipscomb especially troubling. Moore "heartlessly" records Lipscomb's anguish, reported Kermode, who felt "growing revulsion for a film-maker who would resort to such tactics."[11]

As mentioned previously, many critics slammed Moore for creating a strongly biased cinematic presentation. They claimed that the political arguments presented in *Fahrenheit 9/11* were over the top. Moore's messages lacked "nuance," they complained.[12] He did not introduce ideas in a fair and balanced manner. Some movie reviewers writing for university newspapers took this tack, charging *Fahrenheit 9/11* with excessive partisanship. "By definition, a documentary is a film which presents facts objectively without editorializing or inserting fictional matter," declared Andy Thaxton from Texas A&M (Thaxton admitted that he had a limited understanding of the traditions of documentary cinema when he offered that definition). Thaxton called the filmmaker a radical falsifier. "Michael Moore is an extremist," he concluded, "who will go to any length, including telling lies, to further his cause."[13] A reviewer at the University of Texas at Austin took a similar position. Curtis Luciani concluded that Moore demonstrated little interest in nuance and consistency. The filmmaker was "out of his depth" trying to simplify the complex world of geopolitics, said Luciani, and he was trying to serve the public "Noam Chomsky lite" (referring to MIT's radical professor who was known for taking hard-hitting leftist positions on political issues). Luciani observed that Moore had purged from his film record "anything that might force him to refine his argument," calling that practice tantamount to "rhetorical cowardice." Moore, the reviewer claimed, delivered little more than propaganda.[14] Stan Oklobdzija of the University of California at Davis also berated Moore for arguing in the extreme and making a case that rested essentially on emotion. He compared *Fahrenheit 9/11* to *Reefer Madness*, the heavy-handed antimarijuana documentary of 1947 that was a re-release of a 1930s film. Many of today's students of cinema consider *Reefer Madness* a laughable example of ridiculously exaggerated claims.

Some commentators expressed hostility to any form of intensely polemical argumentation, and many (though not all) of those who registered this sort of criticism represented mainstream journalism (and supposed neutrality) rather than the political Right. These commentators often tried to demonstrate that their criticisms of Michael Moore were nonpartisan by complaining about right-wing polemicists too. They warned that radical approaches to political issues stirred the public's emotions but blocked understanding. Americans needed to hear calm and reasonable dialogue, they said, not shouting. Moore's *Fahrenheit 9/11* was too strident, declared Jonathan Foreman. He asked: do we want a Rush Limbaugh standard of political discourse?[15] Similarly, Nick Cohen, writing in the *New Statesman*, declared that Moore's movie was "a sort of Fox News for liberals," suggesting that it stressed only one side of major political arguments.[16]

These concerns about going over the top troubled some supposedly open-minded columnists with the *Washington Post* who declared an interest in criticizing the Bush administration's policies but expressed discomfort with Michael Moore's highly partisan agenda. Columnist Richard Cohen "recoiled from Moore's methodology" because the movie was "a farrago of conspiracy theories." Cohen said that the case against George W. Bush "should not rest on guilt by association," and besides, the movie seemed "prosaic," "boring," and utterly predictable.[17] The *Post*'s William Raspberry confessed that although he agreed with many of Moore's political conclusions, he understood why Republicans hated the film and tried to block its screening. Raspberry was disturbed that a mostly liberal crowd at a Washington, D.C., premiere applauded the movie without restraint. The *Post*'s op-ed writer compared that reaction to the way some middle-class blacks applauded the harangues of radical black nationalist Louis Farrakhan; even though they recognized that some of Farrakhan's facts were probably wrong, they believed "his attitude is right." Raspberry gave little indication of the specific evidence in *Fahrenheit 9/11* that troubled him. Instead, he complained generally about the moviemaker's partisanship. "I wish Moore had been more scrupulously honest, more interested in examining other points of view," said the journalist. He wished that Moore had been "less inclined to make the facts line up to serve his purposes."[18]

Other commentators in the press joined Cohen and Raspberry in expressing disdain for one-sided, over-the-top journalism. Various columnists with liberal, moderate, and conservative credentials reported that they found *Fahrenheit 9/11*'s partisanship troubling. The *New York Times*'s Nicholas Kristof worried that Moore's mud-slinging could further divide the country. President Bush had erred by giving the nation an overdose of moral clarity and self-righteousness, he said, and now Moore was doing the same. Unfortunately, reported Kristof, liberals were cheering Moore's zealotry.[19] Philip Gailey of the *St. Petersburg Times* observed that the election campaign of 2004 was a serious matter, but *Fahrenheit 9/11* was not. Do not trust ideologues of either the Left or the Right, he cautioned readers.[20] Gailey maintained that Americans did not need heavy-handed partisans setting the standard for political discourse in the United States.[21] Charles Williams, in a letter to the *Minneapolis Star-Tribune*, described Moore as an Ann Coulter or Rush Limbaugh of the Left. Was "there no room for compromise?" he asked.[22] Reason and civility are now designated for wimps, complained P. J. O'Rourke in the *Atlantic*. Conservatives have Rush and the liberals have

Moore, O'Rourke reported. He suggested that the name of Michael Moore's production company was revealing: "Dog Eat Dog."

Andrew Sullivan, a prominent neoconservative, articulated an idea that many other critics repeated in subsequent weeks. Sullivan asked whether Michael Moore had become Mel Gibson's "alter ego." Both *Fahrenheit 9/11* and Gibson's movie *The Passion of the Christ* were loaded with cultural bias, Sullivan complained, and both excited gut sentiments. Moore's documentary rallied the faithful of the Left; Gibson's movie stirred the emotions of people on the Right. Each film aroused "various forms of hatred or adoration" by people at the political extremes. Unfortunately, said Sullivan, each film was "deeply corrosive of the possibility of real debate and reason in our culture."[23] Cathy Young also pointed out similarities between *The Passion of the Christ* and *Fahrenheit 9/11* in the *Boston Globe*, as did the liberally inclined on-line magazine *Slate* in a column by David Edelstein, who suggested that Moore was acting like the Left's answer to Ann Coulter.[24]

Among the heavy hitters who slammed Moore for bias were Pulitzer Prize–winning syndicated columnist Ellen Goodman and the *New Yorker*'s well-known film reviewer David Denby. Goodman expressed surprise that people in the theater where she viewed *Fahrenheit 9/11* were not merely watching a movie; they were rooting for it. She asked whether the Left actually wanted its own Rush. Moore's polemics were hardening Americans further into an "us and them" mentality, creating an endless color war between the blue and red states. Goodman suspected that Moore had not persuaded many nonbelievers by taking such an extreme stand. He would do better to reason with people, rather than trying to appeal to their gut, Goodman counseled. Denby, like many other critics, stressed the need for a more balanced and analytical style. He said that filmmakers ought to attempt, "however inadequate, compromised, or hopeless, to arrive at a many-sided understanding of some complex situation." This was clearly not Moore's approach. Moore called himself a "satirist," but a more appropriate term was a polemicist or a practitioner of mocking political burlesque, argued Denby.[25]

Television journalists as well as print journalists joined these reprimands. Their remarks seemed to indicate that Michael Moore had irritated them with his numerous public comments about the media's failures and his use of quotations from them in *Fahrenheit 9/11*. Moore's movie featured several clips from Fox News anchors and reporters, since that network took a particularly gung-ho position on the war with Iraq. But Moore also included remarks from noted anchors of the older news organizations. Dan

Rather of CBS said, "When my country's at war, I want my country to win."
Peter Jennings of ABC offered the confident statement (later proved to be
incorrect) that "Iraqi opposition has faded in the face of American power."
Ted Koppel of ABC's *Nightline* called the American military "an awesome
synchronized killing machine." These remarks, appearing in the context of
Moore's complaints about the media's lack of courage in questioning the
administration's policies, angered the media figures.

Dan Rather did not respond critically to Moore's quotations, but the
leading newsmen at NBC and ABC did. They berated Moore for presenting a highly partisan, one-sided commentary on recent events. NBC's Tom
Brokaw seemed to pinpoint the most important factor behind these intense
reactions: Moore blamed network news for failing to do its job. Moore suggested that the United States had gone to war, in part, because television
newspeople had jumped on the bandwagon led by the Bush administration.
The NBC anchor disagreed with this assessment, arguing that the networks
had given a fair presentation of what they knew at the time. "The American
news networks and the newspapers, for the most part, did as well as they
could under the circumstances," Brokaw asserted. ABC's Peter Jennings
supported that conclusion. When watching *Fahrenheit 9/11*, said Jennings,
he was surprised by "how much ground we'd already covered."[26]

ABC's Ted Koppel echoed the remarks of many other critics when he
suggested that Moore had failed to give balanced news analysis, such as the
networks attempted. Moore is not interested "in getting it straight down
the middle," Koppel complained. The major networks carried related stories about political events but did not present the information in a polemical fashion. "I'm concerned on both sides of the political spectrum that if
what Americans feel they have to get is news with an attitude, what they're
going to end up losing is some of the objectivity that traditionally people in
our business have tried at least." Koppel objected to the notion that Moore's
work could be considered "journalism." *Fahrenheit 9/11* was to documentary
film what the movie *JFK* was to history, Koppel argued.[27] Brokaw joined this
indictment and made an invidious comparison to deliver a similar objection against political bias. The Left has Michael Moore, said Brokaw, while
the Right has Rush Limbaugh. And both polemicists take great liberties
with the facts, manipulating and arranging information to serve their partisan purposes.[28]

While some critics demanded less stridency and more balance in the
treatment of political questions, a few hard-core conservatives thought that

the proper answer to Michael Moore's bombardment from the Left was to design a cinematic attack of their own with right-leaning biases. Three productions attempted to respond to Moore's challenge through the same media: film and video. Publicity for these documentaries, *Celsius 41.11*, *Michael Moore Hates America*, and *Fahrenhype 9/11*, promised that the productions would uncover lies in *Fahrenheit 9/11* and reveal truths. Instead, these films proved to be cinematic exercises in stridency and delivered some of their own myths.

Writer-producers Lionel Chetwynd and Ted Steinberg and director Kevin Knoblock made the sharply partisan documentary film *Celsius 41.11*. They claimed that the title of their film, an obvious takeoff on *Fahrenheit 9/11*, related to the temperature at which the brain begins to die from exposure to the heat of left-wing rhetoric. Chetwynd, Steinberg, and Knoblock received between $750,000 and $1 million from the conservative organization Citizens United to finance their film. Of course, these filmmakers did not promote their production as a biased interpretation. While it was in production, Chetwynd announced, "There will be a high level of scholarship" behind the movie. There would be no "cheap shots" and no manipulation of evidence in the fashion of Michael Moore.[29]

The makers of *Celsius 41.11*, in fact, did manipulate evidence, as do all documentary filmmakers when trying to persuade audiences of the correctness of their cause. The movie's narrative reveals its creators' three principal purposes: to counter several of Moore's major criticisms of the Bush administration in *Fahrenheit 9/11*, to defend President Bush's decision to go to war against Iraq, and to denigrate the presidential candidacy of John Kerry. Several "talking heads" appear throughout the film, each of whom is a notable conservative. These speakers include radio host Michael Medved, actor and former Republican senator Fred Thompson, columnists Michael Barone and Charles Krauthammer, and *Weekly Standard* executive editor Fred Barnes. Their messages are forceful. The speakers report that Michael Moore was terribly wrong in his accusations and evidently thought little of his fellow Americans. The preemptive war against Iraq was necessary and praiseworthy, the commentators stress. George W. Bush's leadership in our time of trial was impressive, and John Kerry is an arrogant flip-flopper who should not be president. In short, *Celsius 41.11* is a hard-hitting partisan documentary (not a "balanced" perspective), which is entirely appropriate in a film that aims to make a strong political statement.

Celsius 41.11 drew only minor attention compared with *Fahrenheit 9/11* because its makers failed to appreciate the insight of one of the early geniuses of American documentary production, David Wolper, whose motto was "information and entertainment," not just information. Wolper recognized that a documentary needed to tell a story dramatically, with a beginning, middle, and end.[30] *Celsius 41.11* lacks that dramatic arc. It pounds viewers relentlessly with information and often appears formless. Unlike *Fahrenheit 9/11*, which rests much of its argument on primary sources (comments from ordinary Americans at home and abroad), *Celsius 41.11* builds its case on the remarks of supposed experts who pontificate about the issues. *Celsius 41.11* is generally humorless. It approaches numerous political topics with weighty seriousness and accompanies its reporting with eerie music that suggests a malicious purpose on the part of Michael Moore (the music seems more suitable for a horror movie). A comparison of the two films suggests the value of Moore's entertaining style for making a complicated story understandable and interesting.

A second documentary from the Right was more amateurishly composed than *Celsius 41.11* but more entertaining. Michael Wilson modeled his film on the techniques employed by Moore. In *Michael Moore Hates America*, Wilson pursues an interview with the filmmaker, much as Michael Moore tried to obtain an interview with GM's Roger Smith in *Roger & Me*. Over the course of this chase, Wilson encounters various American citizens who offer comments on Moore's cinema. Young people with decorative metal jewelry embellishing their faces generally support Moore in these interviews; enterprising Americans who are trying to build their future through hard work in their own businesses (as well as an injured veteran of the Iraq war) criticize Moore's methods. Wilson uses these interviews, as well as his verité-style on-camera appearances, to question arguments made in *Roger & Me*, *Bowling for Columbine*, and *Fahrenheit 9/11*.

Wilson displays promise as a Moore imitator, but he also reveals a sophomoric misreading of Moore's purposes. Wilson interprets Moore's muckraking style as a sign that the filmmaker hates America (he fails to recognize that many social critics want to improve a good society by drawing attention to its shortcomings). Wilson assumes that Moore's criticism of large corporations implies a lack of respect for enterprising Americans who try to lift themselves up through entrepreneurship. The struggling proprietors shown in Wilson's movie are, in fact, the kind of people who are often the subject of Moore's sympathy. Wilson suggests, too, that Moore intended to portray American soldiers as bloodthirsty killers in *Fahrenheit 9/11*. He gives no attention to Moore's claim that the nasty conditions of fighting in Iraq made good young men engage in bad actions. As Moore often pointed out, his target was the war, not the soldiers who had been thrown into it. The silliest criticism of all in Wilson's movie is his berating of Moore, supposed champion of the little man, for becoming rich from his cinematic successes. After celebrating private enterprise and capitalism through much of his film, Wilson tries to cast a suspicious shadow on Moore's ability to advance his personal fortunes by making movies. Whether Wilson expects Michael Moore (or Michael Wilson) to take a vow of poverty after making a popular film that is sympathetic to the "little man" is never clarified.

The third production, Fahrenhype 9/11, is more artistically sophisticated than Celsius 41.11 and Michael Moore Hates America, but its tenor is similar. The movie's key producer is Alan Peterson, a filmmaker who claims to have been a Democrat before the terrorist attacks of 9/11 made him an enthusiast for George W. Bush's policies. He released the movie during the summer of 2004, hoping that it would undermine Michael Moore's claims and promote Bush's reelection prospects. Peterson casts other Democrats, former Democrats, and pro-Republican Democrats (as well as Republicans) as the principal commentators in his cinematic roasting of Moore and his movie. Among the contributors are actor Ron Silver, former New York mayor Ed Koch, Senator Zell Miller, and former Clinton adviser Dick Morris. Silver and Morris receive credit for bringing the production together, and Silver also serves as the narrator. President Reagan's assistant secretary of defense Frank Gaffney, National Review editor David Kopel, and right-wing TV commentator Ann Coulter also make appearances.

If producer Peterson had concentrated on his purported goal of challenging some of Moore's facts, he might have generated a useful debate about the interpretation of evidence in a documentary. For instance, Fahrenhype 9/11 draws attention to Moore's use of a letter to the editor of a Bloomington, Indiana, newspaper and suggests that Moore represented this letter as a news report. In other cases, Peterson's movie counters Moore's criticism of Bush's extensive vacation time by showing that the president was working during his many days away from the White House. Fahrenhype 9/11 reveals, too, that the Oregon state policemen working along the Pacific coast are not primarily responsible for stopping terrorist invaders from the sea; that job belongs to the U.S. Coast Guard. Furthermore, those law enforcement officers are paid by the state of Oregon, so budget cuts by the Bush administration did not significantly affect the number of police officers along Oregon's coast.

Peterson is not satisfied with raising small points, however. He is determined to slam Moore on all issues, and this relentless pursuit leads him into many argumentative traps. After responding to virtually every major claim made in Moore's movie, Peterson's film delivers two principal arguments: that the president's call for military action against Iraq in 2003 was wise and necessary, and that Moore's film communicates a hatred for the United States and disrespect for American soldiers. *Fahrenhype 9/11* concludes by urging patriotic Americans to reject Moore's supposedly vicious and unjust criticisms of the president and the nation.

Zell Miller delivers the pro-war message best when he describes an encounter with a nest of copperhead snakes on his farm. Miller tells the audience that he did not discuss the snake problem at length with his associates or seek assistance from friends. Instead, he grabbed his hoe and chopped off the vipers' heads. The pro-Bush Democrat from Georgia announces proudly that he took "unilateral" and "preemptive" action (as President Bush did when confronting Saddam Hussein). Other speakers accentuate Miller's message by claiming that it is better to fight terrorists in Iraq than at home. In various ways, the speakers describe Saddam Hussein as a serious threat to the United States. They claim that he possessed dangerous weapons, and one speaker describes Saddam as a human "weapon of mass destruction."

With the passage of time, Michael Moore's interpretation of U.S. military engagement in Iraq is much more impressive than the sophomoric, gung-ho, unquestioning saber rattling of the commentators in *Fahrenhype 9/11*. Moore raised doubts (as it turned out, well-founded doubts) about the administration's claims regarding Iraq's possession of weapons of mass destruction and Saddam Hussein's connection to the 9/11 terrorist attacks. The speakers featured in *Fahrenhype 9/11* seem to accept these claims blindly and without question.

Fahrenhype 9/11 also belabors a point that has little relevance to Michael Moore's movie, because Alan Peterson makes an assumption that is essentially false. Toward the end of *Fahrenhype 9/11*, Peterson features numerous commentators who suggest that Moore's film aimed to insult and defame soldiers serving in the U.S. armed forces. An army recruiter claims that his associates promote a *volunteer* force; they do not employ high-pressure sales tactics on potential recruits, as Moore shows in his movie. An amputee who appeared in *Fahrenheit 9/11* claims that he felt violated when Moore used footage from a news report about his personal struggle with his war-related injuries. The injured soldier did not want his story featured in a movie that challenged the necessity of U.S. military involvement in Iraq. Family members and soldiers who lost relatives or friends to military action in Iraq respond tearfully and angrily to Moore, asserting that Americans injured or killed in Iraq loved the United States and believed in the nation's mission. During the final minutes of Peterson's movie, these expressions of anger turn to bitterness. One speaker says that Michael Moore wants to "degrade" American soldiers and make them look "foolish." Another speaker describes Moore as "un-American." Dick Morris offers the final words while swelling, uplifting music accentuates his message. Don't lose faith in the ideals symbolized in the Statue of Liberty, he says (as the camera focuses on the statue). And don't lose faith in yourself.

Like many who blasted *Fahrenheit 9/11*, Alan Peterson treated Michael Moore's interpretation of the president's leadership and his foreign policy as essentially unpatriotic. *Fahrenhype 9/11* implies that Moore intended to disgrace American soldiers and defame the nation. At no time in the film do the narrator or the commentators acknowledge that Moore and other individuals who registered serious objections to the president's policies might be just as patriotic as they consider themselves to be. Moore's critics in the movie demonstrate no awareness of a message promoted by war protesters during the debates about U.S. military engagement in Iraq: "Dissent is the highest form of patriotism."

Critics of *Fahrenheit 9/11* also fail to acknowledge that Moore's attention to the tragedy of Lila Lipscomb, whose son died in the Iraq war, suggests his great concern about the fate of American soldiers. As Moore confirmed many times in public statements, his movie aimed to criticize the architects of the war who worked in Washington, D.C., and recognize the problems that their policies created for American soldiers on the ground in Iraq. When Moore shows those soldiers engaging in controversial activities or expressing doubts about their mission, his purpose is to question the strategies that placed them in these situations, not to depict the men and women of the U.S. armed services as depraved killers. Yet *Fahrenhype 9/11* advances that charge. It suggests that Moore sought to malign the honor of American soldiers. The speakers in Peterson's movie sound very much like those who claimed that critics of the Vietnam War were the enemies of American servicemen. *Fahrenhype 9/11* leaves the impression that Moore's questions about the war in Iraq are intended to disparage the young men

and women who are risking their lives in the effort to bring order and democracy to Iraq.

Peterson's movie, with its sophisticated production values and promised
attention to facts, could have become the most distinguished entry of the
video responses to *Fahrenheit 9/11*, but it finished like the other productions
in the anti-Moore genre. It did not look like a serious documentary about
important issues. The filmmaker's relentless personal attack on the creator
of *Fahrenheit 9/11* left the impression that *Fahrenhype 9/11* had been designed
primarily to shore up the Republican base and ensure that Moore's film
would not damage the president's 2004 reelection campaign.

Partisans of the Right also responded to *Fahrenheit 9/11* through their
Web sites, which contained plenty of biting commentary about Moore and
his film. The criticisms in these venues were blunt and often irrelevant.
Mooreexposed led its presentation with this question: "Should a 400 pound
man advise us on the evils of over-consumption?" Complaints about the
filmmaker's wealth followed. *Mooreexposed*'s writer observed that Moore
promoted himself as a champion of the working class but lived in Manhat-
tan and had another beachfront home in Michigan. In both locales, Moore
resided close to America's elite, and he sent his children to a private school.
David Bossie's site, *CitizensUnited*, reported that Moore got rich making propaganda films that advanced his America-hating agenda.

Some of these Web sites, which were strongly recommended to readers by various conservative writers, featured abundant electronic links, yet
many of these apparent sources of information were of little value. For example, one of the popular references, Dave Kopel's "59 Deceits of 'Fahrenheit 9/11,'" featured a lengthy attack on Moore's commentary about the
flight of Saudi nationals from the United States shortly after September 11,
2001. A link in this Web site to the Associated Press contained no information. A link to Jack Tapper's interview with Michael Moore brought up
the statement, "You've requested an ABC News.com page that does not exist." Another link called National Public Radio led to an especially nasty review of the movie by NPR's Saturday morning host Scott Simon.[31] Whereas
Moore's Web site and book, *The Official* Fahrenheit 9/11 *Reader*, featured numerous references to primary sources—news reports, informative articles,
and other documents—Kopel's links (when they actually led anywhere) often referred readers to opinion pieces that contained little specific historical information.

Some attacks from the Right were presented with much greater sophistication and poignancy and therefore made a stronger impact on public discourse. One of the most influential commentaries, cited often in various articles and reviews in the electronic media, came from the New York Times's David Brooks, who had also served as editor of the conservative Weekly Standard and a contributor to the Atlantic. He listed many statements that Michael Moore had made in recent years in European countries about America and Americans. One of these comments in particular received considerable coverage in the national press after Brooks brought the words to light. During an interview with the Mirror, a British newspaper, the filmmaker said, Americans "are possibly the dumbest people on the planet." Moore told the paper, "We don't know about anything that's happening outside our country. Our stupidity is embarrassing." In an open letter to the German public that appeared in Die Zeit, Moore asked, "Should such an ignorant people lead the world?" In making these harsh statements, Moore had been expressing his frustration over the American public's relatively quiet acceptance of foreign policies that he considered badly mistaken. Nevertheless, Moore's lively characterization of the problem of American acquiescence did not play well back at home. Brooks's compilation of quotations left the impression that Moore was a radical and an extremist who did not think much of his own country and people. Just as Moore had used the words of President Bush and other Republican leaders to ridicule their ideas, Brooks cleverly employed Moore's own language against him.[32]

Christopher Hitchens's comments received considerable attention, too, because he had been a writer for the Nation earlier in his career and had been popularly associated with the Left. Hitchens, ever the master of hyperbole when indicting works of art and politics, sounded very much like William F. Buckley (but working from a different perspective). It is not surprising that Buckley, a longtime conservative editor at the National Review, cited Hitchens's observations on Fahrenheit 9/11 in his column. Buckley reproduced the most-quoted paragraph from Hitchens's stinging analysis and then accented the message by saying, "Get it?" In that damning review, Hitchens said:

To describe this film as dishonest and demagogic would almost be to promote those terms to the level of respectability. To describe his film as a piece of crap would be to run the risk of a discourse that would never again rise above the excremental. To describe it as an exercise in facile crowd-pleasing would be too obvious. *Fahrenheit 9/11* is a sinister exercise in moral frivolity, crudely disguised as an exercise in seriousness. It is also a spectacle of abject political cowardice masking itself as a demonstration of "dissenting" bravery.[33]

Hitchens combined this colorful language with a list of specific objections to the film's assertions. Like many critics, however, Hitchens concentrated on small details and did little to challenge the filmmaker's fundamental thesis. He largely ignored Moore's treatment of the Bush administration's efforts to turn the public's fear of al Qaeda into an unnecessary war with Iraq. Instead, Hitchens stressed that the Saudi government had been opposed to the removal of the Taliban regime in Afghanistan (and thus was not always doing the bidding of its friends in the Bush family). Hitchens pointed out that the 9/11 Commission and antiterror specialist Jonathan Clarke had contradicted Moore's claims about the Saudis' flight from the United States shortly after September 11, 2001. One of Moore's clips that showed a vacationing George W. Bush included British prime minister Tony Blair in the background; thus, Hitchens inferred, the president was not relaxing when he was away from the White House (as Moore had suggested). Like many other critics, Hitchens complained about the movie's treatment of prewar Iraq. He declared that Iraq was not a "sovereign nation," and Saddam Hussein certainly did not rule over a peaceful kingdom during three decades of evil Baathist domination. Furthermore, terrorists such as Abu Nidal and Abu Mussab al-Zarqawi had been welcomed in Baghdad, so Saddam Hussein evidently did have a link with terrorists. In all, said Hitchens, Moore had left out everything that would have given his narrative a problem and included any "rubbish" that supported his preconceived thesis. "You have betrayed your craft," he scolded.

Hitchens's early and oft-cited analysis of *Fahrenheit 9/11* anticipated the explosion of negative evaluations that soon followed. Like Hitchens, these detractors tended to stay away from Michael Moore's principal thesis—that the Bush administration had exploited the public's fear after 9/11 and driven the country toward an unnecessary and counterproductive war with Iraq and occupation of the country. Instead, the detractors pointed their sights at smaller targets. They challenged the movie's claims that the Bush family acted in the Middle East primarily out of financial interests, questioned the movie's perspective on Iraq's history, and complained about Moore's imagery that purported to portray the war's impact on the Iraqi people.

They also objected strongly to the movie's portrayal of activities by U.S. servicemen and questioned the manner in which Moore screened interviews. Through these and other complaints, the detractors slashed around the edges of Moore's arguments rather than stabbing at their center.

Many critics complained that the first third of the movie seemed to accuse both Presidents Bush and many of their close and powerful friends of secret deal making for personal profit. *Fahrenheit 9/11* showed cozy associations between the Bush family and the House of Saud, as well as Bush family ties to other oil-rich Saudis. MSNBC's counterterrorism analyst Roger Cressy claimed that Moore performed a "disservice" when he looked into the Bush family's personal relationships with Saudi leaders, especially when the filmmaker suggested that those economic ties were driving U.S. policy. Claims that the Bushes acted primarily out of concern for their personal profits rather than the nation's interests seemed "wrong" and "unfair."[34] Moore's film also suggested that George W. Bush and fellow Republicans had welcomed the Taliban to Washington because they were interested in supporting Unocal's plans to build a gas pipeline across Afghanistan. According to Andrew Sullivan, the movie implied that the United States had engaged in war in Afghanistan and Iraq "only to enrich the Bush family with oil money."[35]

Many commentators who raised these objections pointed to the provocative language Moore used in the film. In the narration, Moore asks whether the war in Afghanistan was really about the gas pipeline that Unocal executives wanted to build there. Critics insisted that the United States had engaged in combat in Afghanistan because of al Qaeda and the Taliban, not because of the business interests of Dick Cheney or the Bush family.[36] They also objected to the movie's link between Saudi Arabia and the Bush administration's interests. As Hitchens noted, the Saudi government opposed, rather than supported, regime change in Iraq.[37] A conspiracy of interests such as the one Moore implied did not exist, the critics declared.

Moore's claims depended on circumstantial evidence, suggestion, and innuendo, they protested. The movie seemed to imply that President George W. Bush, his top administrators, and his family were involved in conspiratorial behavior. Yet *Fahrenheit 9/11* offered no coup de grace, no masterful summation that tied the many supposedly suspicious elements together, said the critics. Moore "spins outlandish conspiracy theories," declared Jason Zengerle in the *New Republic*.[38] MSNBC's Lisa Myers also expressed disappointment that the film was "heavy" on conspiracy suggestions.[39] Others charged that details in the movie were flat-out wrong. For instance, the pipeline plan for Afghanistan had been abandoned in 1998, they said, so it could not have played a role in the Bush administration's post-9/11 thinking.

Critics of the movie objected strongly to its brief treatment of conditions in Iraq before and after U.S. bombing commenced on March 19, 2003. They expressed disgust with the pleasant images Moore used to represent Baghdad before the U.S. attack. He showed children playing and getting haircuts and adults enjoying lunch at a café and participating in a wedding. Ugly scenes of rocket explosions over downtown Baghdad followed, and Moore showed pictures of badly injured Iraqi civilians, including children. *Fahrenheit 9/11* featured pictures of Baghdad in ruins and its dead citizens. But where was Moore's coverage of the evil government in Iraq that had made the war necessary, the critics asked? They were especially angry about Moore's narration during this segment of the film: "On March 19, 2003, George W. Bush and the United States military invaded the sovereign nation of Iraq—a nation that had never attacked the United States. A nation that had never threatened to attack the United States. A nation that had never murdered a single American."[40] Didn't Saddam Hussein run a police state in the country, critics asked? Wasn't his government guilty of the cruel oppression, torture, and murder of many Iraqi citizens? "This was a genocidal, fascist regime that hated us and was working against us in the most foul way," declared Hitchens.[41] Hadn't Iraqis killed Americans in the Gulf War of 1991, Hitchens queried? Didn't they shoot frequently at American planes patrolling the no-fly zones over Iraq in the 1990s? Didn't Saddam Hussein try to kill President George W. Bush's father? Didn't Iraq harbor Abu Nidal, a terrorist who tried to kill Americans? The University of Texas's film reviewer succinctly captured the spirit of these complaints when he wrote that *Fahrenheit 9/11* "implies that Iraq was utterly harmless."[42]

Quite a few protesters objected to a clip in *Fahrenheit 9/11* showing a wailing Iraqi woman expressing her misery and desperation after a bombing. "They have no conscience!" she cries out. Later she moans, "Oh God! Oh God! God save us from them! Where are you God? Where are you?" But what, specifically, caused the destruction that upset the Iraqi woman, asked the *Wall Street Journal*? The bomb could have come from an errant missile fired by Iraqi antimissile crews. Moore *assumed* that the destruction was due to U.S. military actions.[43] Another critic objected to Moore's report on U.S. servicemen who participated in a Christmas Eve raid that involved breaking into a home and searching it at gunpoint, looking for a young man. Who was that young Iraqi, Tucker Carlson asked? Perhaps he was cooperating with the insurgents or was a terrorist himself. He could have been a sniper who was shooting at American troops.[44] Moore's video coverage of the raid could not answer this important question. Indeed, the young Iraqi might have been working with the enemy.

Another detail from Moore's narrative and interpretation received considerable critical attention in the national media: the charter flights taken by Saudi nationals shortly after the attacks of September 11. *Fahrenheit 9/11* suggested that leaders in the Bush administration had facilitated the quick exit of these foreigners, protecting them from serious questioning about their possible connection to al Qaeda members. Critics took issue with Moore's reporting. They claimed that most of the Saudis who traveled on those planes had been screened by the FBI, and the chartered flights took off *after* U.S. airspace had been reopened. Richard Clarke, the nation's terrorism czar, had given the green light for the flights, seeing nothing wrong with them. Furthermore, twenty-two of the twenty-six bin Ladens had been interviewed before they left. Moore acted as if he had caught the Bush administration red-handed in an act that favored the Saudis and the bin Laden family, but the whole matter was just as Clarke described it: a tempest in a teapot.[45] The 9/11 Commission agreed, these critics noted. Commission members indicated in their report that there was nothing unusual about the situation. Six flights had evacuated 142 people, mostly Saudis, including some from the large and wealthy bin Laden family, but this happened after U.S. airspace had reopened. Several Saudis were interviewed by the FBI, the critics noted, including most members of the bin Laden family.[46]

When Michael Moore made an appearance on George Stephanopoulos's ABC News program around the time of *Fahrenheit 9/11*'s release, he came under attack over another detail: his handling of on-the-street interviews with members of Congress. Stephanopoulos appeared as eager to ambush Moore as Moore had been eager to pounce on the unsuspecting politicians. The ABC host badgered Moore with questions about the response of Mark Kennedy, one of the congressmen Moore had approached in Washington, because Kennedy's remarks had been omitted from the movie. Stephanopoulos claimed that Kennedy had told Moore about having two nephews in the military, one of whom was in Afghanistan. In fact, said the ABC host, in response to Moore's request for help in urging congressmen to commit their own youngsters to military service in Iraq, Kennedy had said, "I'd be happy to, especially those who voted for the war." Stephanopoulos further badgered Moore by noting that critics thought that he hated the United States and was unpatriotic. Because the host constantly hammered at his guest for these supposed discrepancies, the filmmaker had little chance to make his case in the interview.[47]

CNBC's Matt Lauer also seemed eager to spring a surprise on Moore when the filmmaker appeared on his program. Rather than exploring Moore's main thesis about the U.S. responses to terrorism and Iraq, Lauer, like many other commentators, concentrated on small details in the movie that were tangential to the war issue. He reminded Moore of Richard Clarke's statement about the Saudis' flights: "I take responsibility for it. I don't think it was a mistake and I'd do it again." This comment was not in Moore's movie, observed Lauer, yet it appeared in Clarke's book. The omission seemed glaring to Lauer. The host also lambasted Moore for collecting video evidence showing American GIs abusing Iraqi prisoners. Yet Moore had not presented this evidence to the military authorities, Lauer protested, and he demanded to know why not. Scolding his guest, Lauer recited a familiar expression: "If you're not part of the solution, you're part of the problem." He also threw a rhetorical question at the filmmaker, asking, "Do you see yourself as part of the solution?"[48] As in the interview with Stephanopoulos, Moore seemed constantly on the defensive in this unrelenting assault on the integrity of his filmmaking.

Quite a few pundits were angry about the disturbing images of U.S. servicemen displayed in Fahrenheit 9/11. Moore's movie showed them enjoying hard rock music to prepare themselves for combat, and it showed the terrible death and destruction resulting from U.S. bombing and gunfire in Iraq. The movie portrayed American servicemen as trigger-happy buffoons, complained Republican strategist Jack Burkman. "There was banter in the tank," noted Burkman. That scene represented "a deliberate attempt to make fun of American soldiers."[49] Tucker Carlson took a similar position, noting that Fahrenheit 9/11 "makes American soldiers and marines look like animals." The conservative TV commentator maintained that the movie "makes our soldiers look like beasts."[50]

Lauren Burke, reviewing Fahrenheit 9/11 for the Associated Press, joined the pile-on. Burke chastised Moore for citing suspicious evidence. He had confused correlation with causation and supposition with evidence, Burke charged. The filmmaker's extraordinary claims gave his movie an "air of fantasy," said Burke, who concluded with a sharp indictment. Fahrenheit

9/11 "places Moore squarely on the growing list of charlatans and hucksters engaged in a steady business pawning off their fabrications on an unfortunately credulous public," said the reviewer.[51]

Burke's damning remarks were not unusual. Many, though certainly not all, of Moore's critics employed tough language to point out supposed failings. Much of this negative commentary emerged from the word processors and mouths of conservatives, Republicans, and advocates of the Bush administration's policies. Other negative responses came from offended journalists and media pundits, as well as from citizens who wrote letters to newspaper editors in protest against Moore's movie. Many of the complaints stressed the problem of partisanship, arguing that Fahrenheit 9/11 presented an unbalanced, biased, and unfair critique of the president and his policies. In the aggregate, these complaints amounted to an angry rejection of the movie and its creator. The harsh reviews left the impression that Michael Moore's faults were not minor; in fact, critics described them as quite serious. The man and his movie appeared to lack credibility. Fahrenheit 9/11 seemed worthy of dismissal as a grossly partisan and highly distorted interpretation of recent events.

Was Fahrenheit 9/11 truly so bad? Had the filmmaker committed egregious errors in dealing with the facts? Did he fail to give the president and his policies a decent hearing because of his extreme partisanship—indeed, his intense loathing for the president he was studying? Did Michael Moore owe the American people a fairer and more balanced presentation of evidence—something straighter and more down the middle, as Ted Koppel had recommended?

4 The Partisan Documentary

This chapter addresses the question of Michael Moore's partisanship. Since many of the blistering criticisms of *Fahrenheit 9/11* as well as Moore's earlier films focused on their one-sided, opinionated nature, the issue of *committed documentary* (a term often used by film scholars) deserves special attention. This chapter places Moore's cinema in the larger context of documentary filmmaking through a brief excursion into the history of documentary production since the 1930s. That record suggests that Moore did not create a uniquely partisan style of filmmaking. Instead, he made some impressive contributions to a long-standing and evolving practice of agenda-driven cinema.

The familiar claim by many of Moore's critics that his documentaries (including *Fahrenheit 9/11*) ought to present detached, balanced, and thoroughly nonpartisan treatments of history and politics ignores the history of the genre. Critics who insist on strict standards for documentary production promote a limited definition of the term *documentary*. They characterize these films as objective, reportorial interpretations of issues. There are, however, many different documentary traditions, and the sharply partisan form that Moore follows is similar to a technique employed by many other documentary artists. A look at the record of filmmaking over the twentieth century reveals that important practitioners of the craft engaged in opinionated filmmaking well before Michael Moore released his first production.

When asked to imagine the characteristics of a typical documentary film, Americans often conjure up impressions of a rather bland nonfiction movie that presents information in a realistic, objective, and balanced fashion. A good documentary, they expect, is one that shows "both sides" of a controversy so that audiences can develop their own opinions about the issue under study. A fine production supposedly provides viewers with lots of essential details that they need to make personal judgments about current events. The Fox News motto, honored in advertising if not in practice, communicates this ideal succinctly: "We report; you decide." Fox's language deceivingly suggests that its reporters maintain neutrality.

Notions about the impartiality of documentary films derive, in some degree, from misleading terminology. *Documentary* is the generally accepted term that both the public and film professionals employ when discussing the genre. The word implies, on its face, that the makers of these productions comment on evidence dispassionately and document their reports with plenty of facts. The word's origin can be traced to the nineteenth century, Philip Rosen points out, when authorities talked about the "documentation" of evidence.[1] In modern times, references to documentary film suggest an educational purpose, and commentators on these productions often assume that the artists behind them aimed to instruct audiences through a balanced and objective demonstration of evidence.

In many respects, the public's idea of neutrality as a standard for documentaries is a false one, since every action in the production experience requires filmmakers to make judgments. By selecting particular photographs, film clips, interviewees, music, and other elements that go into a production, an artist necessarily promotes a point of view. The artist also creates an interpretation by connecting these elements. Filmmakers influence the audience's opinions by selecting and arranging "facts." Documentary makers juxtapose pictures and words or create a narrative thread for their stories. They deliver messages through the narration of a host or through information imparted by means of interviews. Usually filmmakers leave many feet of interview material "on the floor," choosing to employ only a small percentage of the information obtained from "talking heads," and only that which serves their purposes. These important choices shape a film's messages, making all documentary films "biased" in varying degrees.

Notable and acclaimed film series that appear on American television contain biases, too, even though they appear to provide broad, informative overviews of large historical subjects. Sometimes those opinions are transparent, and other times they are presented in more subtle ways, but the interpretive spin is significant nonetheless. Each film has a thesis; each communicates a specific perspective. *Victory at Sea*, a famous television series of the 1950s about U.S. Navy operations in World War II, offered a gung-ho, patriotic report on the achievements of the U.S. armed services. *Vietnam: A Television History*, PBS's highly praised documentary series of the 1980s, appeared to offer an encyclopedic and objective overview of the war, yet its imagery and interviews communicated opinions. Programs in the series tended to support the conclusion that the United States' engagement in Vietnam had been a terrible mistake (interestingly, conservative groups sponsored production of a counterdocumentary that challenged the inter-pretations offered in this series). In the 1990s Ken Burns's excellent popular series *The Civil War* appeared to offer a balanced and comprehensive over-view of the nation's greatest domestic crisis, yet its nine programs com-municated historical interpretations, too. Burns's programs argued that slavery had been the principal cause of the Civil War, and they reflected the sensitivities of Americans in the post–Vietnam War era by accentuating the tragedies resulting from military conflict.

These three acclaimed historical film series provided opinionated views of the past, even though they were marketed as fair-minded and objective overviews of history, and there is nothing inherently wrong with spinning an interpretation. Indeed, many viewers appreciated these films because they offered strong-minded perspectives. Viewers generally enjoy nonfic-tion films that communicate clear, strong messages. They want to be both informed and aroused. Cinema that offers no principal interpretation or suggests many conflicting ones frequently lacks audience appeal.

Most notable documentaries deliver hard-hitting, assertive perspec-tives because they have evolved from a journalistic tradition that originated with provocative revelations delivered to the public in print rather than on film. Long before motion pictures entered the sound era, society's critics were writing books to stir the public's anger. These discontented scribes sought to excite readers' disgust over corruption, injustice, and human suf-fering. In the early twentieth century, for example, muckrakers drew atten-tion to the problems of the industrial age. Ida Tarbell discussed John D. Rockefeller's manipulative business practices in *A History of the Standard Oil Company* (1904). Some documented their accusations through fiction based on fact, such as Upton Sinclair's *The Jungle* (1906), an upsetting report on conditions in Chicago's meatpacking plants. Years later, John Steinbeck employed fiction to comment on the plight of Americans who lost their homes and farms during the Great Depression. *The Grapes of Wrath* (1939) viewed hardship from the perspective of those victims. In many respects, Michael Moore was a modern-day heir to this long-standing tradition of calling attention to society's tragic stories.

When film historians identify the most significant documentary produc-tions of the twentieth century—the ones that aroused considerable public in-terest and established new techniques that inspired other filmmakers—they usually point to motion pictures and television programs that could be char-acterized as left wing. This does not mean that the artists were, necessarily, radicals or followers of an extreme left-oriented ideology. Rather, in this case, the term *left wing* suggests that the films had, as we say, an "edge." They challenged convention, criticized leadership, attacked powerful interest groups, and questioned authority. Left-wing cinema exposed injustices. Its stories often favored the "common people"— the poor, the working classes, and the middle-class victims of corporate greed or abuse by those in positions of power. Filmmakers' targets were often business moguls and prominent politicians whose actions proved harmful to the masses.

Michael Moore owed a large debt to the many such artists who preceded him. These pioneering filmmakers added to the growing tradition of partisan documentary production. Notable contributions to the development of committed documentaries came from foreign artists such as Joris Ivens (Netherlands), Dziga Vertov (Soviet Union), Luis Bunuel (Spain), and Santiago Alvarez (Cuba), yet many American artists also employed nonfiction film in imaginative ways to expose social problems and launch sharp political critiques. Moore drew from these innovations when he produced *Roger & Me* and his subsequent films, including *Fahrenheit 9/11*. As mentioned earlier, he also received help from two accomplished practitioners of strongly partisan nonfiction documentary, Kevin Rafferty and Anne Bohlen, when designing his first movie.

Scholars who have examined the history of documentaries argue that commitment to a point of view has been fundamental in the activities of many documentary filmmakers. Persuasion is one of the four principal purposes evident in the work of prominent creators of documentaries, argues Michael Renov, an insightful interpreter of the form. Many artists try to promote public debate and ignite political change through their films, Renov notes.[2] He sees the rallying of support for social movements as "a crucial documentative instinct."[3] Bill Nichols, another insightful contributor to film theory and history, observes that documentaries typically provoke and encourage responses from audiences. The makers of these films try to shape attitudes and question popular assumptions, says Nichols. "Arguments about the world" constitute the "organizational backbone of documentary." Filmmakers often appeal to the audiences' emotions, notes Nichols, through alarming cinematic reports on injustice, inhumanity, and barbarism.[4]

In his useful study of the growth of a documentary tradition in the 1930s, William Stott observes that filmmakers who made important contributions in the Depression era approached their subjects with a passionate interest in provoking social change. These artists wished to convince viewers of a need for major improvements in society. They appealed to the sympathies of audiences and tried "to shape [the public's] attitude toward certain public facts." Documentary makers had "an axe to grind," concludes Stott.[5] They wanted viewers to take stands and to "fix things." He acknowledges that many of these documentary productions constituted a form of "propaganda." But that term can be misleading, Stott points out, because it often carries strongly negative connotations. Commentators typically think of disturbing examples of film propaganda from the 1930s, such as Leni Riefenstahl's *Triumph of the Will*, which glorified Adolf Hitler and his Nazi Party. Yet there is "honest propaganda," too, argues Stott. Several documentary films of the 1930s aimed to persuade in socially responsible ways.[6]

Pare Lorentz's *The Plow that Broke the Plains* (1936) is a particularly important American documentary of that era, and some film scholars consider it "honest propaganda." The film took controversial positions on important public issues. Lorentz sought to enlighten the American people about significant environmental problems in the nation's Farm Belt. With financial support from an agency of Franklin D. Roosevelt's New Deal administration, he produced a documentary with a strong thesis, intelligent narration, and impressive music to support his film's point of view. *The Plow that Broke the Plains* identified actions of people and the government that had contributed to a tremendous drought in the prairie region of the country. The movie looked and sounded like a brief in favor of Roosevelt's farm policies and his plans to have the federal government take the lead in dealing with troubles in the Dust Bowl. Not surprisingly, various opponents of the New Deal denounced the film as promotional cinema that amounted to a not-so-subtle endorsement of the Democratic president's administration. Critics complained that taxpayers' money should not be funneled into such controversial projects. Some citizens of the prairie states objected to the movie because it appeared to depict their region as a ruined wasteland.[7]

During World War II, General George C. Marshall turned to a filmmaker when he sensed that the U.S. Army faced a morale problem. Marshall believed that many recruits had been influenced by antiwar sentiments. They needed some prodding to excite their contempt for the enemy and to sharpen their understanding of the issues underlying the conflict. General Marshall was convinced that "to win this war we must win the battle for men's minds." To do so, he turned to noted Hollywood director Frank Capra. Capra managed the development of several documentary films in a series called Why

We Fight. The first movie in the series contrasted the ideas and actions of totalitarian regimes with those of democratic societies. Capra and his colleagues skewed the evidence heavily in favor of the Allies' cause. They cleverly used sounds and images to argue that the United States was a land of freedom, whereas Germany, Italy, and Japan were frighteningly tyrannical societies. Films in the Why We Fight series did not have the appearance of balanced, nonpartisan works of cinematic art, but many Americans who watched them in the early 1940s probably would have agreed with Stott's observation that such films represented commendable examples of essentially "honest propaganda."

Emile de Antonio was one of the most important artists of the postwar era who introduced techniques that Michael Moore would later employ. Politically, de Antonio was a highly committed radical partisan and took antiestablishment stands in each of his movies. He is most famous for creating *Point of Order* (1963), a documentary film about the confrontation between the U.S. Army and Senator Joseph McCarthy in 1954. The production features scenes from the famous televised hearings that explored McCarthy's charges about communist influences in the army. McCarthy made a fool of himself in these exchanges, and de Antonio's film gives the senator adequate cinematic "rope" to hang himself by showing some notable moments in which the demagogic politician attacked individuals unfairly. The filmmaker does not provide an overall narration in *Point of Order*. Instead, de Antonio juxtaposes cinematic evidence in ways that send a strong critical message about McCarthy's malicious behavior.

De Antonio's other notable films were transparently partisan, too. *In the Year of the Pig* (1968) criticized America's involvement in Vietnam. *Millhouse* (1971) skewered Richard Nixon. *In the King of Prussia* (1982) displayed sympathy for antinuclear protesters who had been arrested. *Mr. Hoover and I* (1989) raised questions about FBI director J. Edgar Hoover (whose organization had harassed de Antonio because of his connections with radical causes). Like Michael Moore, Emile de Antonio introduced humor and satire in his films, although he did not give himself a central on-camera role, as Moore did.[8] De Antonio could make viewers laugh at the foibles of the people under study (as in his examination of Nixon in *Millhouse*). Like Moore, he injected humor in his productions not only for purposes of entertainment but also to make viewers think.

In the 1970s, documentaries about women, including productions with a feminist perspective, also contributed to the growing tradition of committed nonfiction filmmaking in the United States. Often these films mixed sympathy for blue-collar workers and women. *Union Maids* (1976) recorded the experiences of three female workers in the textile and meat plants of Chicago who put in long hours under difficult conditions for low pay. The production by Jim Klein, Miles Magulescu, and Julia Reichert suggested that the people under study were struggling for equality in a manner that resembled later fights for women's and workers' rights in the United States. Barbara Kopple released *Harlan County, U.S.A.* the same year. Her documentary provided a hard-hitting analysis of a violent strike in Kentucky's coal mines. Kopple's sympathies were clearly with the male miners and the women who supported them during the strike. Two years later, three women produced *With Babies and Banners: The Story of the Women's Emergency Brigade*, a documentary about the work of hundreds of women who backed the famous autoworkers' strike at the General Motors plant in Flint, Michigan, in 1937. The strike helped establish the United Auto Workers union as the bargaining agent for blue-collar workers in the plants. *With Babies and Banners*, created by Lorraine W. Gray with help from Lyn Goldfarb and Anne Bohlen, also favored the laborers' perspective. Then, in 1980, Connie Field released *The Life and Times of Rosie the Riveter*. This frankly feminist movie displayed sympathy for the women who moved from the kitchen to the factory during World War II, providing American industry with much-needed workers. Field then showed how the manufacturers pushed these women out of their coveted jobs when the fighting came to an end, to make room for the returning war veterans. All these notable documentaries of the 1970s and early 1980s about blue-collar workers and suffering but strong women offered keenly partisan perspectives.

Major contributors to developments in documentary cinema also experimented with innovative formats prior to Michael Moore's appearance as a filmmaker. Frederick Wiseman became one of the leading practitioners of a form called cinema verité, in which the creator abandons narration, interviews, and soundtrack music in an effort to get closer to the action with a more natural recording of events. Wiseman's documentaries, filmed during the last decades of the twentieth century, studied injustices prompted by the exercise of power in U.S. society. Among his subjects were an institution for the criminally insane, a high school, a hospital treating the poor, a basic training camp for military recruits, and an Episcopal monastery.

Some documentary artists use other films as a source or object of their commentary, and Michael Moore evidently imitated some of their techniques.

In 1982, Jayne Loder, Kevin Rafferty, and Pierce Rafferty explored this technique impressively with a darkly comic film, *Atomic Café*. They gathered archival footage that had been filmed with a serious intent and edited it to display the information humorously. Specifically, *Atomic Café* combined old training and demonstration films so as to raise serious questions about the United States' testing of nuclear weapons in the 1940s and 1950s. Likewise, Peter Davis and Bert Schneider experimented with diverse video sources in an innovative way in their 1975 Academy Award–winning documentary *Hearts and Minds*. Davis and Schneider juxtaposed diverse evidence, such as news footage and interviews, to create a sharp indictment of U.S. military actions in Vietnam. In several sections of *Fahrenheit 9/11*, Moore employed archival film and interviews related to the war in Iraq in a similar manner. Like the makers of *Atomic Café*, Davis and Schneider omitted the seemingly omniscient voice of a narrator and depended on the original source material and interviews to deliver their message.

Some innovative documentary filmmakers of the late twentieth century incorporated elements of dramatization within a nonfiction format. Since film footage was not available to illustrate each important aspect of a story, they employed dramatic representations to fill in some of the gaps. Errol Morris designed a notable example of this technique with *The Thin Blue Line* (1988). He staged dramatic depictions to question evidence that had placed an apparently innocent man in prison (the movie helped win his release). Some of these dramatic elements were quite brief in duration (for instance, Morris showed a milkshake dropping in slow motion). His use of "fictional" elements aroused a good deal of controversy but also paved the way for further experiments in this type of hybrid documentary—a combination of the factual and the fictional. Although Moore did not employ this technique in his movies (except indirectly in his comedy routines, such as the one about the Coalition of the Willing), it became increasingly evident in the work of various other artists by the late twentieth century.

There were also experiments with amusing but significant behind-camera appearances by a narrator, a technique that Moore has applied throughout his documentary work. Ross McElwee gained considerable media attention for employing this strategy three years before the appearance of *Roger & Me*. In *Sherman's March* (1986) McElwee placed himself through narration at the center of a documentary film that was supposedly about the famous Union general's progress through the South during the Civil War. Instead,

McElwee devoted much of his storytelling to a highly amusing account of his travels through Dixie, including his romantic encounters with a number of interesting women. McElwee's camera also offered some fascinating insights into the unique people and culture of the modern American South.[9]

As film theorist Bill Nichols has pointed out, this cinematic approach, in which the artist makes statements in a first-person voice, transparently signals to the audience that the documentary is designed to look more like a personal essay than a supposedly objective, balanced, nonpartisan presentation. The appearance of a filmmaker's commentary in a production (along with his body, as in Moore's films) clearly shows that the material under question is offered as a personal perspective. This technique gives artists an opportunity to suggest that their interpretation *represents* reality rather than *reproduces* it, says Nichols.[10]

This technique can also be judged more honest and candid than the traditional reportorial documentary style in which a seemingly omniscient "voice of God" narrates the story, as if the filmmaker's interpretation is the unassailable truth. A traditional reportorial design conceals the fundamentally subjective nature of documentary projects, whereas the on-camera appearance of an artist such as Moore suggests the personal nature of the enterprise. Filmmakers make numerous judgments in the course of the creative process. At every turn in the production of a film they make choices that can affect, directly or indirectly, the messages delivered to audiences. Documentary productions are not truly objective, no matter how much their promoters advertise them as such,[11] and Moore's technique brings that interpretive quality to the audience's attention.

Those who have examined the history of the documentary are emphatic in disagreeing with those who promote the traditional view that nonpartisanship is a sine qua non of documentary production. Film scholars recall that one of the pioneers of the documentary, John Grierson, defined the form as "the creative treatment of actuality," and subsequent practitioners of the craft have emphasized the word "creative." Modern-day students of the genre stress the persuasive character of documentaries, referring to them as a form of "committed" filmmaking. Documentaries stand somewhere between art, entertainment, and journalism, argues Pat Aufderheide, director of the Center for Social Media at American University.[12] They aim to raise questions about serious issues, promote public education, and excite viewers to take social and political action. The role of a documentary is "to ask the hard, often disturbing questions so pertinent to our age," comments Alan Rosenthal, editor of an important survey of the genre, *New Challenges to Documentary*.[13]

Michael Moore seemed to reflect this perspective when he defended himself against claims that he took a heavy-handed approach to interpretation. Moore's critics tried to apply an old broadcast standard when scolding him for partisanship. Just as the Federal Communications Commission once required the major networks to provide "equal time" for individuals to defend themselves against political attacks, Moore's critics demanded that he address controversial issues with a sense of balance.

Moore responded to this oft-repeated criticism by saying that he had never intended to engage in dispassionate reporting. *Fahrenheit 9/11* was not supposed to serve as a cinematic example of front-page news reporting, said Moore. "My films are a work of journalism," he explained, "but they're journalism of the op-ed page." Moore argued that his job "is not to present all sides. My job is to present my side." *Fahrenheit 9/11* offered *opinions* about the first years of George W. Bush's administration, Moore acknowledged, and he welcomed debates about those judgments.[14] Moore said that critics should not expect disinterested commentary in his films, any more than they should expect detached commentary on the editorial page of a newspaper. "I'm not trying to pretend that this is some sort of fair and balanced work of journalism," Moore insisted.[15]

Moore and his defenders were quick to point out that the Bush administration had not been "fair and balanced" in its promotion of the war in Iraq. In speeches and information released to the media, the administration had presented the evidence in a manner that strongly supported its position. Commentators on the news then promoted these biased perspectives through their outlets in the press, radio, television, and the Internet. Figures such as Matt Drudge of the *Drudge Report*, Robert Novak and Charles Krauthammer of the *Washington Post*, and radio and TV personalities Sean Hannity and Bill O'Reilly eagerly broadcast interpretations of the news that supported the Bush team's spin on events. Were those commentators supposed to abandon their practice of delivering opinions on the news?

Moore identified his partisan film as a legitimate journalistic enterprise and a particularly needed response to the network news's cowardly reporting on President Bush's foreign policy. The villains in *Fahrenheit 9/11* were not just Bush, Cheney, Rice, Rumsfeld, and other foreign policy activists, nor Drudge, Novak, Hannity, and other super-enthusiasts of the Right's causes in the national media. Moore maintained that the traditional news sources—major newspapers and radio and television news organizations—failed to protest loudly when the Bush administration tried to advance its controversial policies. These organizations allowed the president's publicists to manipulate the news by reporting the administration's version of events without objection.[16] Leaders in the White House and the Pentagon "successfully got the networks to drink the Kool-Aid," Moore complained—an obvious reference to the followers of cult leader Jim Jones who had calmly and without protest committed mass suicide by drinking the poisonous concoction served to them.[17] Supposedly respectable members of the mainstream media were not doing their job, Moore argued. In the film, Katie Couric's exclamation that "Navy Seals rock!" hints that she was acting like an unwitting contributor to the administration's propaganda schemes.

Moore found the media's failure to question the Bush administration's official claims about its actions in Iraq similar to their acquiescence to government propaganda in the days of the Vietnam War. Until the late 1960s, television news networks in the United States gave considerable attention to the government's official pronouncements on the war and offered relatively little protest against it. Moore, who grew up near the Canadian border, recalled watching Canadian reports about the Vietnam War, "and it wasn't what Americans saw." TV viewers in the United States were kept in the dark largely because of these journalistic shortcomings. In the present, Moore recognizes a similar failure to ask tough questions. "They're not showing these things on TV in America," he said, referring to the war's impact on citizens, soldiers, and Iraqis. The filmmaker from Flint intended to present a contrasting vision in his movie.[18]

Many of those who criticized Moore's partisanship demanded that he show the "other side" of conditions in Iraq before the war began. As mentioned previously, Moore's detractors were angry that he featured cheerful scenes of the pleasant conditions in Baghdad shortly before the bombs began to fall in March 2003. Critics complained that Moore offered no information on the terrible crimes of Saddam Hussein and no commentary on the oppression and intimidation suffered by those supposedly happy Iraqi people under the regime of the evil dictator. Baghdad was not Paris in 2003, they argued.

Not surprisingly, Moore considered these charges ridiculous. "Who doesn't know that Saddam was a bad guy?" he asked. Network television had promoted that message constantly in its reports. Moore wanted to give viewers a different perspective on the situation in Iraq, one not typically covered in the news broadcasts. He included twenty seconds of images showing Iraqi children in a barbershop and flying a kite and adults getting married and enjoying lunch in a café. Those scenes suggested that many victims of the bombing of Baghdad were ordinary citizens who shared the same desire for peace, security, and a good life that Americans sought.[19] Those twenty seconds of images challenged viewers to imagine the consequences of a massive bombing attack on San Diego or St. Louis or Atlanta.

When viewed in the context of broad developments in documentary production in the United States and abroad, Michael Moore's penchant for producing hard-hitting, opinionated, "committed" films is not extraordinary. Although his critics accused him of doing something new that violated the traditional standards of objective documentary interpretation, Moore was actually operating well within the documentary tradition when he made *Fahrenheit 9/11* and other strongly opinionated movies. If there was anything strikingly "new" about his activities, it was his demonstration of unique skills in marketing and promoting his film to the public and in turning himself into a nationally famous celebrity. Moore advanced the craft impressively by showing that the cinematic artist could be a funny and enormously entertaining on-camera persona, but he certainly did not invent a new form of partisan documentary. In crafting *Fahrenheit 9/11*, Moore drew on advances made by the numerous pioneers of nonfiction cinema who came before him.

Michael Moore in interview mode for *Roger & Me* (1989).

An advertisement for Michael Moore's *Bowling for Columbine* (2002).

Michael Moore pauses
during the shooting of
Bowling for Columbine (2002).

Michael Moore at 75th Annual Academy Awards festivities, holding his Oscar for
Bowling for Columbine, which won for Best Documentary Feature.

Posters for *Fahrenheit 9/11* (2004).

Michael Moore with Jay Leno on the *Tonight Show* (October 15, 2004).

Lila Lipscomb and Howard Lipscomb, Sr., parents of Sgt. Michael Pedersen of Flint, Michigan, who died in Iraq. From *Fahrenheit 9/11* (2004).

President George W. Bush issues a warning to terrorists, and then adds: "Now watch this drive." From *Fahrenheit 9/11* (2004).

A sweat-stained President George W. Bush driving the golf ball off its tee. From *Fahrenheit 9/11* (2004).

President George W. Bush shouts at Michael Moore (off camera): "Behave yourself—go find real work." From *Fahrenheit 9/11* (2004).

Michael Moore on Capitol Hill, speaking with Congressman John Tanner (D-Tennessee). Moore asked Tanner and other congressmen who supported the Iraq War if they would recruit their own children to go fight in that war. From *Fahrenheit 9/11* (2004).

Michael Moore with Sgt. Abdul Henderson recruiting on Capitol Hill. From *Fahrenheit 9/11* (2004).

Marine recruiters speaking with teenagers outside a shopping mall in Flint, Michigan. From *Fahrenheit 9/11* (2004).

President George W. Bush continues with the reading of *The Pet Goat* in a Florida elementary school for nearly seven minutes after learning that two planes had hit the World Trade Center in New York City on September 11, 2001. From *Fahrenheit 9/11* (2004).

5 Let the Debate Begin

Michael Moore had two main purposes when he made *Fahrenheit 9/11*. The first, as he said in an interview at the time of the movie's release, was to raise questions about the Bush administration's policies that had gotten the nation into a war with Iraq. "Let the debate begin," he said, challenging the American public and the national media to consider the many questions he had raised in the film. Moore's second key purpose was to get practical results from his cinematic provocation. As he indicated during the promotional tour, he hoped to arouse enough anger and action to help push President George W. Bush and his entourage out of Washington, D.C. The filmmaker thought that his production would contribute significantly to the defeat of Republicans in the 2004 elections. This chapter considers the role of *Fahrenheit 9/11* in advancing that debate about the nation's political course, and the next chapter explores the movie's impact.

Fahrenheit 9/11 is, essentially, two movies rolled into one, and in some respects, Michael Moore's strategy resembles that of a boxer planning for a big match. During the first half of the entertainment, Moore throws punches in numerous directions, attempting to draw blood from the public corpus of George W. Bush. His goal is to pummel the president's image of dignity and credibility. Moore hopes that the first hour of cinematic assault will undermine the president's reputation for inspired leadership. The filmmaker tries to make Bush look like a staggering and limping figure rather than a heroic icon. Moore does not expect to deliver a knockout punch in the first half of his production, but by asking lots of questions, he expects to soften the audience's impression of the target. Then, in the second half of this "match," Moore tries to strike his opposition with hard and direct blows. The final portion of the film, much more focused than the first, punches strongly at the president for leading the nation into a mistaken military and administrative intervention in Iraq. In short, the first half of *Fahrenheit 9/11* is playful; it contains lots of humorous quotes and scenes that lampoon Bush and the members of his policy team. The second half employs some of these entertaining techniques as well, but the tone becomes more serious. In the final minutes of the film, Moore goes for the knockout blow, allowing his key interviewee, Lila Lipscomb, to do the punching for him.

Why did Michael Moore pursue this storytelling strategy? The less directed, shotgun approach taken in the first hour allowed Moore to address many different controversial questions without settling them. The filmmaker raised numerous doubts about the Bush team's actions, and Moore provided abundant "facts" about these topics, but he could draw no firm conclusions about any of these debates through a presentation of compelling evidence. There was insufficient time in the movie to pursue each topic satisfactorily. In the case of each subject under study, Moore could point to the *appearance* of smoke without producing a smoking gun. Indeed, Moore would have had to devote the full two hours of his movie to just one of these subissues if he intended to give his audience a sense of comprehensive analysis.

A number of segments in the first half of *Fahrenheit 9/11* could have served as attractive subjects for lengthy exploration in a documentary film (such as the type offered in PBS's distinguished series *Frontline*). Pertinent topics include the following:

1. The manner in which disputes about the presidential election of 2000 were settled.
2. George W. Bush's activities at his Texas ranch and in other locales in the months before 9/11.
3. The Bush family's relationship with wealthy and powerful Saudi Arabians.
4. The influence of the Carlyle investment group.
5. The Bush administration's handling of warnings about terrorism prior to 9/11.
6. The flights of Saudi nationals out of the United States shortly after the 9/11 tragedy.
7. American economic interests in Afghanistan and Iraq.
8. Controversies about the Patriot Act, including the federal government's investigation of a group called Peace Fresno.
9. The nation's preparation for dealing with terrorist attacks after 9/11, and the Bush administration's reasons for employing a color-coded warning system.
10. The panicked state of many Americans over the threat of terrorism.

11. The nation's lack of readiness to deal with terrorists because of budget squeezes, exemplified by a shortage of state troopers responsible for guarding the Oregon coast.

Moore raised so many questions about these diverse subjects that some commentators in the national media assumed he was enamored of conspiracy theories. They suggested that the filmmaker found unseemly behavior around every corner. Critics blasted Moore for relying on dubious evidence and using innuendo to suggest wrongdoing.

Yet Moore was only raising questions about these matters, and they were usually justifiable ones. As Moore stated, "I'm just raising what I think is a legitimate question . . . I'm just raising a question."[1] In almost every case, the evidence that Moore presented to arouse distrust of the Bush administration was not incorrect (though some of his angry detractors claimed it was). Rather, that information was subject to interpretation and debate. Defenders of the administration could dispute details in the film by offering other evidence. Or they might judge the meaning of Moore's "facts" in a different manner. In nearly every instance, though, Moore drew attention to information that deserved further exploration. He was correct when he stated that he was just raising "a legitimate question."

Probably the most criticized story-within-the-larger-story in the first half of the movie concerned the departure of Saudi nationals after 9/11, and the record on that subject resembles the nature of the disagreements on many themes addressed in Fahrenheit 9/11's first hour. Moore's evidence on this topic deserves attention, as do the points raised by his critics. Regarding the broader matter of the significance of this dispute, Moore stands on the higher ground. He never maintained that he could answer all queries about the topic; rather, his intention was to highlight issues that deserved greater attention in the national media.

Fahrenheit 9/11 points out that in the days following September 11, 2001, all commercial and private airline traffic had been grounded, leaving many Americans stranded because of this national emergency. Yet 142 Saudis, including 26 members of the large bin Laden family, were able to leave the United States by air within a few days of September 11. Moore relies on testimonials from three individuals to suggest that these Saudis received special treatment and probably should not have been allowed to exit the country so quickly. Craig Unger, author of a book about the relationship between the Bushes and the Saudis, notes in the movie that one of Osama bin Laden's sons got married in the summer of 2001 in Afghanistan, and several bin Laden family members showed up at the wedding.[2] Unger implies that some of these family members may have been privy to information that would have helped U.S. authorities track down Osama bin Laden. Retired FBI agent Jack Cloonan (a senior agent on the joint FBI-CIA al Qaeda task force) supports Unger's concerns by arguing that he (Cloonan) would have wanted to hand out some subpoenas to get those Saudis "on the record" about what they knew concerning Osama bin Laden. Finally, Senator Byron Dorgan of North Dakota supports Moore's probe of the flights by asking, "What happened?" Dorgan wants to know "How did it happen? Why did it happen? And who authorized it?" The senator asks for a "significant investigation." Thus, Moore cannot prove that the Bush administration intervened on behalf of the Saudis, including members of the bin Laden family, but he strongly implies that the administration provided assistance and allowed some potentially useful interviewees to leave the United States too quickly.

Critics, both Republican spokespersons and news commentators, protested loudly about *Fahrenheit 9/11*'s treatment of the Saudi flights. These detractors concentrated on details of the case rather than the broader implications of Moore's presentation. As mentioned previously, they claimed that there was no evidence that the flights took place before the reopening of national airspace on September 13. Several Saudis had been interviewed and screened by FBI agents, the critics pointed out, including twenty-two of the twenty-six members of the bin Laden family. The FBI concluded that these foreigners were not individuals "of interest." Richard Clarke, the president's antiterrorism specialist at the time, acknowledged that he had given the clearance for these people to leave the United States and believed that he had been correct in doing so. Furthermore, the 9/11 Commission's report indicated that the flights were not improper. Hence, Moore's supposed revelation was apparently just a tempest in a teapot. There was nothing inappropriate about the flights, say the detractors, and by giving those flights such emphasis, Moore displayed a penchant for conspiracy theories.

Who was telling the truth in this dispute? Information contained in hundreds of references to this topic that appeared in news sources in 2003–2004 is quite varied and often contradictory. Some of the "facts" seem to support Moore's thesis. Other evidence appears to undermine it. Thus, anyone who speaks with unmitigated confidence in rendering a judgment on the basis of this conflicting published information is feigning a grip on the truth.

The public record, especially the one that was available to Moore at the time he made his movie, did not provide sufficient evidence to slap a seal on the file indicating "Case Closed."

Moore constructed his argument about the Saudis' flights on the basis of investigations by Craig Unger, who reported on the topic in an October 2003 article in *Vanity Fair* and in the opening pages of his 2004 book *House of Bush, House of Saud*. The *Vanity Fair* article, reproduced in Moore's *The Official Fahrenheit 9/11 Reader*, takes the position presented in the movie: the Saudis had close personal and economic ties with the Bush family and received White House support when George W. Bush's friend, Saudi ambassador Prince Bandar (affectionately called Bandar Bush by the Bush family), sought a quick exit for the Saudis.[3] *Fahrenheit 9/11* features a comment Bandar made to Larry King. The prince says, "with coordination with the FBI we got them all out." Moore concedes that the flights occurred after U.S. airspace had reopened and with FBI approval, but he maintains that some domestic flights arranged to collect the Saudis from around the country prior to their international trip occurred *before* the U.S. government's ban on nonmilitary flights had been lifted.

Did the Saudis, including the bin Ladens, receive special treatment during this national emergency? Did highly placed individuals in Washington intervene to honor Prince Bandar's request? Moore's critics place great emphasis on the 9/11 Commission's report, which judged the flights legitimate and proper, but the carefully worded report was not fully credible. The bipartisan commission consisted of a balanced mix of Republicans and Democrats, and the commission had to phrase its findings cautiously in an election year. Under those conditions, the commissioners were not likely to use damning language that berated the Bush administration for allowing the Saudis, particularly the bin Ladens, to leave the United States in haste. Republican members of the commission were unlikely to sanction a wrist-slapping exercise, recognizing that such a reprimand could emerge as a major topic in the presidential debates. The 9/11 Commission's report was, after all, a political document as well as an educational one. It pointed fingers at various agencies of the federal government for failing to anticipate and prevent the terrorists' attacks, but it did not lay blame in any significant way on the man in the White House. Nor could any commissioner realistically expect it to do so under the circumstances.

Furthermore, the 9/11 Commission report concentrated on the limited question of whether suspected terrorists may have been on those flights, whereas *Fahrenheit 9/11* raised much broader questions. The 9/11 Commission reported that the FBI had interviewed all persons of interest who traveled on those planes and "concluded that none of the passengers was connected to the 9/11 attacks and have found no evidence to challenge that conclusion." Wrote the commissioners, "Our independent review of the Saudi nationals involved confirms that no one with known links to terrorism departed on these flights." A footnote supporting that statement provides information about the "TIPOFF" terrorist watch list (there were no matches connecting the passengers to suspected terrorists).[4]

Because Moore's film did not simply argue that terrorists may have escaped on those flights, the 9/11 Commission's limited commentary and conclusion are of little value in assessing the arguments made in *Fahrenheit 9/11*. The commission did not directly address or attempt to answer the questions Moore raised in his movie. The commissioners did not adequately investigate the role of Bush administration officials in securing the Saudis' quick exit shortly after 9/11, and they did not adequately discuss whether those Saudis could have provided information to assist in the hunt for Osama bin Laden.

A view above this complicated forest of details, arguments, and counterarguments reveals that the fundamental questions raised by Michael Moore were significant and deserved consideration. Even though the FBI interviewed several of the departing Saudis, those discussions were evidently quite limited, given the rushed circumstances. During the chaos and confusion immediately after 9/11, there was little chance for a probing discussion with family members concerning their knowledge of Osama bin Laden's whereabouts (or the location of other members of al Qaeda). Perhaps some of those Saudis would have been able to identify people in Saudi Arabia or elsewhere who could provide leads. They may have been able to offer clues about the sources of Osama bin Laden's financial support. In the critics' effort to challenge Moore's credibility, many of them failed to recognize the broad implications of their arguments. They defended the rapid exit of members of the bin Laden family just a few days after the 9/11 crisis, even though Osama bin Laden was at the top of America's most wanted list, and even though the Saudis were a potential source of useful information about the events of 9/11—far more useful than the hundreds of other foreigners who were questioned or detained in connection with the 9/11 probe. Disputes about flights, statements, dates, and clearances were not nearly as relevant as this essential matter, which was directly addressed in *Fahrenheit 9/11*.

In 2005 Gerald Posner published *Secrets of the Kingdom: The Inside Story of the U.S.-Saudi Connection*, a lengthy and detailed probe of U.S. links with Saudi Arabia over the years. Posner made the issue of the Saudi flights central to his effort to raise suspicions about the concealing of evidence, suggesting that assurances provided to the American public by the FBI and the 9/11 Commission could not be trusted. "The 9/11 Commission gave the Saudis a free pass," Posner concluded. "This book shows why."[5]

Evidently, Moore had good reason to raise serious questions about the Saudi flights, yet his treatment of this complex issue in *Fahrenheit 9/11* was brief, and it could have been clearer. Numerous clips, interview segments, and scene cuts amount to a choppy and incomplete indictment of the Bush administration for defending those flights. Moore never suggests the identity of the individuals in the Bush administration who supposedly intervened on behalf of the Saudis (but neither did anyone else who investigated the matter). Also, Moore sometimes mixes references to the bin Ladens and to Osama bin Laden quite loosely. The multibranched bin Laden family, associated with a huge construction company, is among Saudi Arabia's most successful and prominent families, and from all appearances, the ideas of many family members are dramatically different from those of "black sheep" Osama. Some of Moore's language in the film suggests a form of guilt by association based on family surname. Moore could have clarified his presentation by staying closer to his basic argument—that lengthy interviews with the bin Ladens over many days might have led to valuable tips for tracking down Osama.

These shortcomings need mention, but they certainly do not support the scathing indictments issued by Republicans and some commentators in the national media. Those critics acted as if Moore had made outrageous and, indeed, mendacious statements concerning the flights, when in fact he had merely raised questions about some news reports that remained the subject of intense dispute well after his movie appeared. Moore did not present a fictional story about the Saudis' quick exit from the United States; he featured one side's argument in a legitimate conflict of interpretations. The dispute was not easy to resolve because of the fragmentary evidence available in the public record.

During the first hour of *Fahrenheit 9/11*, Moore did indeed slip into language that could easily get him into trouble. Had he stuck with the presentation of intriguing visual and aural evidence (the primary sources) and avoided efforts to summarize in a provocative way, he might have encountered less criticism.

Moore could not resist the temptation to make pointed suggestions, however, and he paid a price for his audacity.

For instance, Fahrenheit 9/11 reported in considerable detail about the Bush family's close financial and personal ties to the Saudi royal family and its oil interests. Few critics objected to the specific information in this coverage, since it had been documented through many news stories. The movie's attackers did, however, protest Moore's interpretation, which suggested that these financial connections seriously compromised President George W. Bush when he dealt with Middle Eastern issues. Moore tried to undermine the president's image as the premier defender of American interests. The filmmaker hurt his case by summing up this message in an especially provocative way. Moore asked, "Is it rude to suggest that when the Bush family wakes up in the morning they might be thinking about what's best for the Saudis instead of what's best for you and me?" Many viewers thought that the question was, indeed, rude. Moore had already made his case against the president with impressive evidence, and his risky concluding observation seemed too blunt and damning. It invited criticism, whereas the collection of interviews and imagery that immediately preceded the question communicated ideas with greater subtlety and power.

Another controversial statement from the first hour of the movie involved the visit of Taliban members, who stopped by the State Department in March 2001. The filmmaker mentions that Unocal Corporation planned to build a gas pipeline across Afghanistan, and Halliburton (formerly headed by Dick Cheney) was scheduled to obtain a drilling contract at the pipeline's Caspian Sea location. Moore suggests that the Bush administration's two-month delay in starting the war in Afghanistan in 2001 may have been related to these economic interests. (Critics maintain that the pipeline deal had been scratched in 1998 and did not play a role in the administration's planning.) When Moore asks, "Was the war in Afghanistan really about something else?" (i.e., not the pursuit of Osama bin Laden), he wades into unnecessary controversy. Moore does not have the evidence on hand to make his point persuasively, whatever it is.

Americans understood and supported the Bush's administration's fundamental reason for invading Afghanistan: to pursue al Qaeda. Both Republicans and Democrats eagerly endorsed that action. In some sections of Fahrenheit 9/11, Moore seems to share that view, even berating the Bush administration for delaying the invasion of Afghanistan. On this matter, Moore appears to stand on firm ground. He raises legitimate questions about the two-month delay after 9/11, which may have allowed Osama bin Laden and his associates to escape from Afghanistan. Presidential candidate John Kerry raised the issue of this delay several times during the 2004 campaign, especially in the televised debates with Bush. Kerry argued that the United States' number-one enemy got a two-month head start because of the president's tardy action and because the Bush administration depended on members of Afghanistan's Northern Alliance to serve as proxy fighters. Perhaps Osama and his supporters could have been caught if the technically sophisticated U.S. forces had handled most of the war-making task instead of the more primitively equipped and less effectively organized Afghan soldiers. Yet Moore took the punch out of this indictment by making the United States' war in Afghanistan sound like a sleazy affair performed in the interest of powerful investors who wanted to build a gas pipeline.

Moore's emphasis on President Bush's financial interests was not inappropriate, for the major arguments in his movie paralleled some of those made by Kevin Phillips in an important book published around the time of *Fahrenheit 9/11*'s release. In *American Dynasty: Aristocracy, Fortune and the Politics of Deceit in the House of Bush*, Phillips traced familiar charges that the Bush administration engaged in crony capitalism and militarism. Phillips, a wayward Republican who achieved distinction for publishing several well-documented, populist-style assaults on economic privilege, found evidence to support the familiar charges. He cast a critical eye on the Bush family's overt and covert financial ties. Phillips maintained that George W. Bush's favoritism toward companies such as Halliburton and Enron resembled the favoritism of family predecessors toward other preferred corporations, including those in the defense and energy industries. The author described a web of covert international relationships during the vice presidency of George H. W. Bush, for instance, and he noted the Bush family's close ties to the Saudi royal family. In many respects, *American Dynasty* provided documentation for a discussion of several issues raised fleetingly in the first half of *Fahrenheit 9/11*.[6]

On many other topics raised during the first hour of the film, protesters either were silent or could manage only to throw puffballs at Moore. Their relative silence may have been related to the paucity of evidence available to defend their positions. These other issues could not be attacked as easily as Moore's points about the Saudi flights, the Bush family's ties to the Saudis, its favoritism toward corporations such as Halliburton, and its supposed interest in a pipeline in Afghanistan. Thus, critics challenged a number of other accusations made in the first hour of *Fahrenheit 9/11* with flimsy arguments or left them relatively uncontested.

For instance, critics objected to Moore's suggestions about a stolen presidential election in 2000, noting that studies by nonpartisan organizations and the news media indicated that the vote counting in Florida was correct and that George W. Bush was, in fact, the winner. These detractors were correct on the technical point, but *Fahrenheit 9/11* identified many other controversial matters about the election that continued to excite debates long after the 2000 election. The film notes that John Ellis, Bush's first cousin, served Fox News on election night and made the first network call that gave Florida to Bush. *Fahrenheit 9/11* reminds audiences that the votes of many African Americans were discounted in Florida and that Katherine Harris, the chairperson of the president's reelection campaign in Florida, was in charge of authorizing the votes for her state. The film points out that some conservatives on the Supreme Court interpreted the Florida vote-counting dispute in a manner that helped put George W. Bush in the White House. Moore could not produce evidence clearly indicating that Al Gore belonged in Washington instead of Bush (who could?). Nevertheless, he was able to raise enough poignant questions to underscore a point that many Democrats were still making at the time of the movie's release. The manner in which Republicans had won the Florida vote dispute still aroused considerable suspicion, even in 2004.

Regarding other jabs taken by Moore in *Fahrenheit 9/11*'s first hour, Republicans attempted to punch back but landed no serious blows. For example, *Fahrenheit 9/11* indicated that, based on a *Washington Post* report, the president had been on vacation 42 percent of the time during his first eight months in office prior to September 11. Not fair, cried the critics. A trip to the Texas ranch or Camp David or Kennebunkport was not necessarily a leisurely vacation. The president worked away from the White House as well as in it, they insisted. Besides, in one of Moore's clips of a supposedly vacationing president, Tony Blair can be seen in the background, and discussions with the British prime minister were surely not devoted only to fishing, hunting, or golfing.

This argument is soft, because Moore gives screen attention to that perspective. He shows George W. Bush saying, "They [people who might accuse him of not working hard] don't understand the definition of work, then." The president insists, "I'm getting a lot done." Bush explains that he need not stay in Washington to handle his responsibilities as chief executive. In a time of telephones and faxes, a leader can accomplish a great deal when working away from the office. Moore thus anticipates his critics' response. Furthermore, his attention to the president's fondness for vacations is not designed merely to make him look lazy; this message is relevant to Moore's broader thesis. By questioning the president's absences from Washington and his vacation activities in the summer of 2001, the filmmaker suggests that the president did not take seriously the intelligence warning he received on August 6, 2001, about possible al Qaeda strikes against the United States.

Moore's point is important, and it received a good deal of attention in the analyses of how the United States had been caught by surprise on September 11, 2001. Less than five weeks before that date, on August 6, the president received a disturbing report in his daily briefing. It contained the shocking title, as Condoleezza Rice acknowledged in the film, "Bin Laden Determined to Attack Inside the United States." The report warned of the possible hijacking of planes by terrorists, yet the president remained in a vacation mode, and his associates did not respond in an appropriate manner, in view of the developments on September 11. In this context, the questions raised by Moore about the president's leisure activities do make sense.

Timothy Naftali's judicious review of the history of U.S. intelligence failures in dealing with terrorism, published the year after Fahrenheit 9/11's release, suggests that both critics and defenders of the Bush administration can find evidence to support their cases regarding the August 6 report to the president. Facts that Moore presented in his movie appear in greater detail in Blind Spot: The Secret History of American Counterterrorism. Naftali shows that leaders in the Bush administration were preoccupied with building a nuclear defense shield and other issues during the late summer of 2001. They did not pay adequate attention to warnings submitted by Richard Clarke and others about threats from al Qaeda and Osama bin Laden. The president's lack of responsiveness to the August 6 report was just one of many disappointing reactions by principals in the administration to the growing threat of terrorism. Yet Naftali, who compiled a report for the 9/11 Commission, also identifies the failures of people in the Clinton administration, and he shows that various FBI and U.S. military personnel missed valuable opportunities to take actions that might have averted the tragedy of 9/11.[7]

Naftali's informative narrative on the question substantiates a point made at the beginning of this analysis. Many of the disputes about Moore's arguments in Fahrenheit 9/11 involve the interpretation of facts, not whether the facts themselves are correct. Moore chose to accentuate evidence of the U.S. failure to deal with terrorism in a way that made the Bush administration look bad. Others could interpret that same evidence in a way that distributed blame for the tragedy in many directions, essentially exonerating the president. Moore presented his "truth" on the subject, and others could challenge it. The debate that Moore promoted in this portion of the film was clearly legitimate.

Critics' complaints about the movie's powerful cinematic assault on the president's reputation as a strong leader—the video footage showing Bush reading to elementary school students for seven minutes after learning that the nation was under attack on September 11—are noticeably paltry and unintentionally humorous. Some detractors offered little more than a "gotcha" correction, observing that the title of the book the president was reading to the class was not *My Pet Goat*, as reported in the film, but *The Pet Goat*. Republican spokespersons, trying to make the best of a difficult situation, claimed that the president had taken the correct action by remaining calm and continuing the reading exercise. They maintained that it would have been a mistake to frighten the children or alarm the public with a hasty response. After all, wasn't that precisely the kind of behavior that many Democrats had complained about—a cowboy mentality that supposedly led George W. Bush to operate on impulse? The president, impressively, did not act like a cowboy on that fateful day, said his defenders. He collected his thoughts and awaited more information. Then, like a firm leader, he acted. The rest is history.

Actually, Moore made history by bringing the president's seeming paralysis to the attention of the American people. No amount of rationalizing or explanation could put that delayed reaction in a good light. The nation was in the midst of a crisis, as White House assistant Andrew Card had made clear when he told Mr. Bush, after the second plane hit the World Trade Center, that the nation was under attack. A fast-thinking president would have concluded that, as the national leader, he was a likely target of the attackers and that, by remaining in the school, he might be endangering the lives of all the children in the building. Besides, important decisions needed to be made quickly (for instance, should the air force shoot down other airliners flying suspicious routes?). Each minute was precious in the crisis. Surely it was not the time to sit with the children as they listened to a story about a pet goat.

Interestingly, despite the multitude of book pages and television and radio hours devoted to the criticizing of *Fahrenheit 9/11*, there is relatively little recorded response to the other important salvos delivered by Michael Moore in the first hour of his movie. Very few commentators reacted to Moore's strong criticism of the way Congress had passed the Patriot Act with little attention to its details, such as the extraordinary powers of surveillance it gave to the U.S. government. Critics said little about *Fahrenheit 9/11*'s consideration of the way the terror alerts left the American people in an extended state of fear. There were noticeably few comments about the movie's attention to the financial and political clout of the Carlyle investment group, even though the film indicated that the Bush family and its associates worked closely with wealthy Saudi investors, including the bin Ladens. Most of the anger registered in print and in the electronic media was expressed about three matters: the movie's treatment of the Saudi flights, claims of ties between the Bush family and the Saudi royal family, and the reporting of a proposed gas pipeline in Afghanistan. Other complaints expressed a general discontent with conspiracy theorizing or communicated disgust for a documentary film that was so strongly opinionated rather than balanced and "objective."

The second and more serious half of *Fahrenheit 9/11* begins abruptly after Moore makes his visit to a state trooper's remote station along the Pacific Ocean. Suddenly, the audience sees President Bush in the final minutes before announcing on television the beginning of the war with Iraq. Then, for a brief time, cheerful scenes of life in prewar Baghdad appear on the screen. Children play. Adults enjoy leisure time at a restaurant and participate in a wedding. Then the audience sees the familiar news footage showing tremendous blasts and fire disrupting the Baghdad night. Bush continues his speech, and subsequently the audience views the apparent consequences of the bombing. A man standing by a pickup truck full of dead bodies holds a dead baby. Within seconds, a U.S. soldier, speaking on a street in Iraq, confesses that "a lot of innocent civilians were killed," and other U.S. soldiers explain how they get "the ultimate rush" when shooting and killing the enemy by listening to a song called "The Roof Is on Fire." These few minutes of coverage were the target of a good deal of the criticism leveled against the second half of *Fahrenheit 9/11*.

Two principal objections dominated these discussions. First, critics protested Moore's seemingly cheerful picture of prewar Iraq, which showed nothing of the violence and oppression that Saddam Hussein practiced against his own people. Moore made the war seem unjustified, they argued, because he portrayed prewar Iraq as a sort of Middle Eastern paradise. Second, these detractors objected to the movie's treatment of American soldiers, saying that these and later scenes made them look like insensitive killers and brutal occupiers. Moore's coverage of the situation in Iraq, they said, insulted the fine men and women of the U.S. armed forces who put their lives on the line every day in that dangerous country.

The angry blasts against Moore's display of happy and peaceful Iraqi civilians reflect an ignorance of the techniques of documentary filmmaking and a strongly simplistic and mistaken view of the message Moore intended to send. The tradition of using sharply contrasting images to shock audiences and arouse their emotions is a time-honored practice in documentary production. As mentioned earlier, Moore often employs the technique by juxtaposing strikingly distinctive images or statements. He is especially skilled at contrasting humorous and serious material in a manner that excites audience interest and thought. In this segment of the film, the humor is somewhat muted, and the contrast between images of peace and war are jolting. As Moore explained, the twenty seconds of film showing happy Iraqi people enjoying life in Baghdad was not designed to conceal the evil of Saddam Hussein's regime. Everyone in the theaters was already familiar with that news story, Moore argued. Network television had not, however, done enough to show what the American bombing and shooting did to the civilian population.

With the passage of time, evidence has emerged that supports the wisdom of Moore's attention to this subject. A few months after the movie appeared in theaters, Americans learned that, according to the best estimates available, Iraqi deaths from the war and postwar troubles may have amounted to more than 100,000.[8] In other words, the president's decision to bring war and occupation to Iraq had had tragic consequences for the people of that country. There were, of course, many causes contributing to the huge number of casualties, including attacks by insurgents and suicide bombers. Yet the chain reaction of violence that tore apart Iraqi society (especially in the region of the Sunni triangle) began with George W. Bush's decision to call on U.S. military personnel to bomb, invade, and occupy Iraq.

Furthermore, Moore's focus on the bombing in Iraq directed viewers' eyes to a matter that had received insufficient attention in the national media. The U.S. armed forces had unleashed hundreds of missiles that went crashing into various sites around Baghdad and other cities. Many of the targets were adjacent to the homes of ordinary Iraqis. *Collateral damage*, the military euphemism for the unintended destruction of civilians' lives, limbs, and property, could not be avoided. *Fahrenheit 9/11* presented Americans with disturbing pictures of those unintended consequences, and it showed, in juxtaposition, Secretary of Defense Donald Rumsfeld saying, "The targeting capabilities and the care that goes into targeting is as impressive as anyone could see." Clearly, the national media were much less likely to question the administration's defense of the bombing of Iraq than Michael Moore was.

Moore's picture of the good life in Baghdad before the bombing began on March 19, 2003, is not *the* truth, but it is *a* truth. There is no single conclusion or appropriate image that comprehensively and adequately portrays prewar conditions. A filmmaker telling a story about oppression under Saddam Hussein might feature images of men in dark cells or scenes of torture chambers or interviews with the victims of a gas attack on a Kurdish village by Saddam's forces. A documentary filmmaker such as Michael Moore portrays happy children and adults to communicate the idea that Iraqi citizens would choose the absence of war if they had a voice in the matter. We cannot know what happened specifically to those apparently healthy, cheerful children, but their on-screen presence symbolically represents the thousands of Iraqi youngsters who must have perished in the violence that shattered Iraqi society in the weeks, months, and years after March 19, 2003. Moore's images remind viewers of the bloody consequences of war.

At the end of the anti-Moore documentary *Celsius 41.11*, pro-Bush filmmakers show happy Americans enjoying the good life. Supported by inspiring background music associated with Thanksgiving are pictures of happy children, cheering crowds at a baseball game, and families enjoying time together. A U.S. soldier appears briefly; he is evidently helping a needy child in a foreign war zone. These images communicate a positive picture of Americans' activities, and that is a legitimate exercise for the producers of *Celsius 41.11*, who wanted to finish their film with an upbeat impression of conditions in the United States and the world during the years of George W. Bush's leadership in the White House. Obviously, some viewers could object to this conclusion. They might claim that many children in America live in poverty, that numerous families have been shattered by divorce, or that in some cases the military actions of U.S. Army personnel inadvertently brought injury or death to Iraqi civilians. Critics could register their complaints, but they would be no more relevant to the discussion than the complaints leveled against Michael Moore for displaying sunny images of life in Iraq before the bombs dropped. Reasonable observers of documentary films recognize that these montages communicate aspects of a story, not the entire story.

Regarding the second major criticism of the second half of *Fahrenheit 9/11*—that the film insulted the hardworking and risk-taking U.S. soldiers in Iraq—Moore's detractors could not be more incorrect. Their accusation blatantly contradicts the filmmaker's thesis. Moore was direct and specific in communicating his principal argument regarding the responsibility of U.S. troops in Iraq. In view of that directness, it appears that some who charged the filmmaker with insensitivity to the plight of U.S. servicemen did not actually view the film, did not pay close attention to its narration, or chose to deliberately misrepresent its message.

Throughout the second half of *Fahrenheit 9/11*, Moore shows that decent young Americans found themselves in confusing and frightening situations in Iraq. They were not the perpetrators of evil in Iraq; they were the victims of mistaken policies that placed them in the line of fire unnecessarily. The errors of planners in the Defense Department and the White House led these soldiers into bad situations in a far-off land, where they did not know the language or the culture or which people they could trust. "You don't really know who's friendly, who's the enemy," says one U.S. soldier. Later in the film another remarks, "The United States was planning on, uh, to just walk in through here like it was going to be easy and all, but it's not that easy to conquer a country." Another soldier describes the danger presented by Iraqi "kids," referring to young men aged seventeen or eighteen. He says, "They hate us. Just why? I'm not really sure." Still another U.S. soldier says that Americans want to "help these people," but the Iraqis seem intent only on convincing the Americans to leave. "I hate this country," he confesses—a succinct statement that communicates a sense of deep frustration. Finally, a soldier describes the emotional impact of the war. "You cannot kill someone without killing a part of yourself," he remarks.

In this portion of the film, Moore offers a thesis that ties these disparate interviews together. He says, "Immoral behavior breeds immoral behavior. When a president commits the immoral act of sending otherwise good kids to war based on a lie, this is what you get."

In one section in the second hour, Moore seems to invite unnecessary controversy (as he did a few times in the first segment), using language that can easily be challenged by the critics. As American bombs begin to strike Baghdad, Moore says, "On March 19, 2003, George W. Bush and the United States military invaded the sovereign nation of Iraq—a nation that had never threatened to attack the United States. A nation that had never murdered a single American." As mentioned previously, Christopher Hitchens and other critics of Fahrenheit 9/11 attacked this interpretation. They pointed out that Saddam Hussein had supported the attempted assassination of George H. W. Bush years earlier and that the Iraqi leader had trained his guns on American troops and equipment during the 1991 Persian Gulf War. Saddam Hussein also ordered his military to fire at U.S. planes guarding the no-fly zone in the 1990s, and he had given sanctuary to terrorists who had attacked American citizens.

Both sides in this dispute are right to an extent—a good reason for Moore to avoid presenting this argument in a way that left it open to contrary interpretation. As many international leaders argued in early 2003, the United States did not have the right to attack the sovereign nation of Iraq, although an unmitigated sanction from the United Nations—which George W. Bush did not receive—would have helped give legitimacy to the coalition's invasion. Furthermore, most of Hitchens's examples of Iraqi aggression against Americans were technically weak. Moore used the word "murder" with the intention of taking the discussion outside of warfare. He knew, of course, that Iraqis had shot at Americans during the Persian Gulf conflict and had fired on U.S. planes when they attempted to maintain the no-fly zone as part of the postwar settlement. Yet these were not acts of "murder" that could be interpreted as directly justifying war. Nor was the presence of Abu Nidal and other terrorists in Iraq a cause for war; in fact, the terrorists that Hitchens and other critics pointed to were typically foreigners, not Iraqis. Finally, Hitchens invited scorn when he mentioned the attempted assassination of President Bush's father to bolster the case for war against Iraqi aggression. That threat against the elder Bush has been documented, but the assassination attempt was certainly not a principal cause for war in 2003. And if it had been, Bush's critics would have had a field day, arguing that George W. Bush had led his nation into battle against Saddam Hussein to avenge the failed assassination attempt against his "daddy."

Thus, Moore's statement is technically correct, but it is not politically correct. The subtleties of phrases such as "sovereign nation" and "never murdered a single American citizen" were easily lost on Americans, who later heard angry pundits denouncing the filmmaker for saying things that could be so easily challenged. Moore had made a strong enough case against the invasion and occupation of Iraq and did not need to employ those provocative "fightin' words."

Although Moore was, understandably, a target for criticism because of the way he handled this topic and others, the achievements of *Fahrenheit 9/11* far outweigh its shortcomings. In fact, the movie's limitations are rather puny in view of the many controversial subjects Moore addressed in the space of just two hours and the numerous sharp insights he offered audiences in that brief time. *Fahrenheit 9/11* is an extraordinary accomplishment in the field of "infotainment." It identifies most of the key criticisms of the Bush administration's treatment of the 9/11 crisis and the Iraq war that came under public consideration in the years before its distribution. Also, the filmmaker collected an extraordinary mix of primary evidence regarding those controversies. His sources—film clips and interviews—identified the essence of political resistance to the Bush administration that was taking shape in 2003 and early 2004. Subsequent developments proved Moore correct on many issues, and national news stories that broke after the film's release confirmed many of the important accusations Moore made in *Fahrenheit 9/11*.

The most important message of *Fahrenheit 9/11* is that the war with Iraq was unnecessary. Near the end of the film, Moore lets a woman in a retirement home articulate this point directly. She asks, "Where are the weapons of mass destruction? It was a . . . we were duped. We were really duped. And these poor people, the young men and women who are being killed there . . . it's unnecessary."

In the months before the war started, as the Bush administration built its case for war in the public mind, George W. Bush, Dick Cheney, Donald Rumsfeld, Condoleezza Rice, Paul Wolfowitz, Colin Powell, and others in the administration referred often to these supposed weapons. Moore shows several of those claims on the screen. Bush says confidently that Saddam Hussein has "taken great risks to build and keep weapons of mass destruction." Powell announces that Saddam Hussein is determined to get his hands on a nuclear bomb. Audiences see the president in various situations saying "nuclear weapon" and "he's got 'em." Yet Hans Blix, the UN arms inspector who headed an inspection team in Iraq before the war, sharply contradicted these claims. During the first months of 2003, the team traveled throughout Iraq, and although Blix's investigators found some old sites of dismantled programs, they uncovered no evidence of current work with weapons of mass destruction (WMDs). Later, Blix said, "We went to sites that were given to us by U.S. intelligence and we found nothing. They said this was the best intelligence we have, and I said, if this is the best, what is the rest?"[9] The lack of proof about WMDs impressed the leaders of UN member nations, and they refused to approve direct military action against Iraq.

In September 2004, nearly a year and a half after the Bush administration led a coalition into war and occupation, Charles A. Duelfer, the top CIA weapons hunter, issued an interim report that confirmed what Blix, David Kay, and other inspectors had concluded: the weapons were not there. Information that Duelfer's team sent to Congress contradicted nearly every assertion made by members of the Bush administration about WMDs in the months before the war began. His Iraq Survey Group had interviewed everyone it could find associated with programs that had ended more than a decade earlier. Then, the group had essentially given up the search, which had cost many millions of taxpayer dollars authorized by Congress. There was no public accounting of the total cost, for the Pentagon's Defense Intelligence Agency indicated that the budget and expenditures would remain classified information.[10] The government's actions left the impression that U.S. taxpayers had funded an expensive search for WMDs not only to secure any existing weapons but also to help the Bush administration find something resembling a threat before the American voters went to the polls in 2004. In short, Moore raised a legitimate concern when he challenged the administration's principal rationale for invading Iraq.

Additional confirmation came in the spring of 2005 when the White House's own Intelligence Commission, headed by Judge Laurence H. Silberman and former senator Charles S. Robb, concluded that U.S. agencies had been "dead wrong" in their prewar assessment of Iraq's nuclear, biological, and chemical weapons. The commission's blistering criticism indicated that the U.S. government's collection of information prior to the invasion of Iraq was "either worthless or misleading." The government's analysis of the threat from Iraq was "riddled with errors." Thus, the United States invaded Iraq on the basis of one of the "most damaging intelligence failures in recent American history." Although this commission hammered the CIA and other intelligence-gathering bodies, it did not broadly address the question of whether officials in the Bush administration had pressured intelligence specialists to find data that could justify a war. This is not surprising, for the president and his administrative team gave the commission a limited mandate. Democratic House Minority Leader Nancy Pelosi complained appropriately that "the investigation will not be complete unless we know how the Bush Administration may have used and misused intelligence to pursue its own agenda."[11]

Michael Moore also reminds viewers that the administration justified the war and occupation by suggesting that Saddam Hussein was closely associated with al Qaeda and Osama bin Laden. Again, Moore uses the president's own words to make the point. George W. Bush asserts, "Saddam Hussein aids and protects terrorists, including members of al Qaeda." Vice President Dick Cheney claims, "There was a relationship between Iraq and al Qaeda." The screen then shows the president mentioning "Saddam" and "al Qaeda" several times in various stump speeches. This example, too, is central to Moore's thesis in *Fahrenheit 9/11*. The filmmaker maintains that the president exploited the nation's fears about the terrorist attacks and mistakenly directed the public's anger toward Iraq, a country that had no direct connection with the events of 9/11. Moore includes a clip in which Richard Clarke, the president's counterterrorism czar, recalls that members of the Bush administration "had been planning to do something about Iraq before they came into office."

These issues identified in *Fahrenheit 9/11* were well documented in reports that came out after the movie was in production. Public opinion polls indicated that at one point after the U.S. invasion of Iraq, 69 percent of the American public believed that there was a direct link between the activities of Saddam Hussein and the events of 9/11. Even in late 2004, toward the end of the presidential election campaign, the percentage of respondents who subscribed to this opinion remained amazingly high—about 40 percent. Polls taken around the time of the election found that Americans who voted for George W. Bush were much more likely to believe that there was a link between Iraq and al Qaeda than those who voted for John Kerry. Clearly, the many comments made by Bush, Cheney, and others in the administration about a supposed Saddam Hussein–al Qaeda connection had an impact on public perceptions. Yet the evidence of such a link was distinctly absent in the months before and after the U.S. bombing and occupation of Iraq. The 9/11 Commission determined in its 2004 report that there was no discernible connection, and most knowledgeable observers concluded similarly.

A great deal of information surfaced in 2004 to confirm Richard Clarke's claim that the Bush team had been strongly interested in military action in Iraq well before the 9/11 attacks. Ron Susskind's book *The Price of Loyalty* revealed that Paul O'Neil, Bush's former treasury secretary, had made that observation. It is also well known that many of the neoconservatives who became Bush's key foreign policy advisers had been lobbying for the removal of Saddam Hussein for years. In *The Official Fahrenheit 9/11 Reader*, Moore reproduces a letter that several of these individuals signed and sent to President Bill Clinton in 1998. They called on Clinton to devise a strategy that "should aim, above all, at the removal of Saddam Hussein's regime from power." They announced that they "stand ready to offer our full support in this difficult but necessary endeavor."[12] Donald Rumsfeld and Paul Wolfowitz, Bush's defense secretary and deputy defense secretary, were among the signers.

In another segment of the film, Moore shows CBS News anchor Dan Rather saying, "Iraq could become, quote, 'another Vietnam,'" and Moore provides evidence of a parallel, based on the growing number of American lives lost. The movie shows various television reporters summarizing those losses: 162, says one; 244, notes another; and the figures climb quickly to 825. Of course, they surged much higher in the months after *Fahrenheit 9/11* reached the theaters.

As American losses climbed, and as the U.S.-trained Iraqi forces appeared unable to maintain security on their own, references to Vietnam grew during the year after *Fahrenheit 9/11*'s release. A *New York Times* article published in January 2005 summarized the concerns of American politicians, military leaders, and citizens. Titled "Flashback to the 6os: A Sinking Sensation of Parallels between Iraq and Vietnam," the article noted that all historical analogies are risky, because the circumstances are always different, yet Americans of the 2000s were worried about many of the same things that had concerned Americans of the 1960s. Senator Edward M. Kennedy observed that in the early days of both the Vietnam War and the Iraq war, Americans believed that they were winning, yet "we did not understand that our very presence was creating new enemies and defeating the very goals we set out to achieve." One of the most relevant parallels, according to the article, was the resemblance between "Vietnamization" and "Iraqicization." In both cases, U.S. military leaders hoped to remove their troops once the local regimes had been trained by Americans and were strong enough to defend themselves. This plan had failed in Vietnam, for the South Vietnamese troops were overwhelmed shortly after U.S. forces left the country, and Americans in the 2000s wondered whether a similar training plan could succeed in establishing strong security forces in Iraq.

The *Times* article identified concerns that were expressed briefly but poignantly in *Fahrenheit 9/11*.[13]

Senator Kennedy's claim that the U.S. presence in Iraq could alienate much of the population is a matter that gets considerable attention in Moore's film. As mentioned previously, Moore shows a U.S. soldier saying that it is not easy to conquer a country, and other servicemen express dismay that there is so much resistance from people they are only trying to help. Why do they hate us, a soldier asks? President Bush provides a clue in *Fahrenheit 9/11* when, in an awkward remark made at a press conference, he says, "They're not happy they're occupied. I wouldn't be happy if I were occupied either." Through these and other quotes, Moore delivers an important message. He maintains that the presence of a foreign army in a distinct culture such as Iraq's—a condition that implies occupation to the Iraqis—has the potential to irritate many of the natives. Americans are there to help the Iraqis, but as Senator Kennedy argued, such intervention can create new enemies and defeat the purposes of a well-intentioned program.

Evidence that continued to emerge from Iraq after the release of *Fahrenheit 9/11* showed the wisdom of Moore's warnings. Numerous commentators on the United States' troubles in Iraq observed that the presence of so many foreign troops and foreign bureaucrats and businessmen in the country, especially Americans, left Iraqis feeling impotent. In an age of nationalism, this massive intervention in Iraq's affairs insulted many Iraqis; it wounded their sense of pride. These Iraqis desperately wished that the foreigners would leave. Other Iraqis were willing to tolerate the American presence a little longer because of the lack of security and the continuing danger from insurgents and suicide bombers, but they remained uncomfortable with the occupation. They understood a disturbing contradiction: although the Americans and other foreigners might provide protection from violence, their continued involvement provoked many people in Iraq and other Islamic countries to participate in a guerrilla war against the American and coalition forces, thus adding to the violence.

Fahrenheit 9/11's coverage of the occupation of Iraq anticipated another major issue that emerged after the movie's release: American soldiers' treatment of Iraqis. Two segments drove home the point. One is the Christmas Eve raid on a Baghdad neighborhood, in which U.S. servicemen kick down the door of a home and apprehend a young man, who is described by a crying woman as a college student. Moore shows the man on his stomach on the floor as American soldiers shine a flashlight in his face. In the other segment, which received a good deal of discussion in the media, Moore shows Iraqi detainees with hoods over their heads. U.S. soldiers are taking photos of them, and one says, "Ali Baba has a hard-on." The soldiers remark that one of them touched the Iraqi in the genital area.

When Moore gathered this material from freelance cameramen, he intended to use it to support his point about bad things happening when a president "commits the immoral act of sending otherwise good kids to war based on a lie." In the months after the release of *Fahrenheit 9/11*, this seemingly minor material in the narrative became quite important.

Abu Ghraib became a household word when Americans learned in 2004 that the large detention center in Baghdad had been the site of numerous abuses, including acts of humiliation, sexual intimidation, and torture carried out by members of the U.S. armed forces. Shocking photographs revealed naked detainees with leashes around their necks, one with a hood covering his face and wires connected to his body, and another naked man hunched over with his arms outstretched, evidently in fear of a large black dog being restrained by an American soldier. A report by investigative journalist Seymour Hersh and his subsequent book documented many of these outrages. Mark Danner also reported in detail on these problems in the *New York Review of Books* and in his own book-length publication.[14]

These reports revealed that in many cases the abuse of prisoners began when men were captured and shipped to the U.S. base in Guantanamo, Cuba. There, at least, there were many guards available to work with the prisoners. In Iraq, however, the prisons held thousands of people rounded up in broad sweeps, many of whom were evidently just unlucky bystanders. In the crowded U.S. holding facilities, the prisoner-to-guard ratio was seventy-five to one, and the management and training of the American guards appeared inadequate.

Furthermore, the Bush administration had pushed for a legal redefinition of torture after the 9/11 tragedy. Alberto Gonzales, later Bush's choice for attorney general in his second term, played a significant role in orchestrating these changes. The administration loosened the rules for interrogation. Vice President Dick Cheney explained the need to do so, saying that Americans had to work "sort of on the dark side. A lot of what needs to be done here will have to be done quietly, without any discussion, using sources and methods that are available to our intelligence agencies, if we're going to be successful."[15] Gonzales sent a memo to the president in early 2002 that described some points in the Geneva protocols as "quaint" and "obsolete." By August 2002, assistant attorney general Jay Bybee informed Gonzales that the president was within his legal rights to permit American interrogators to inflict "cruel, inhumane, or degrading" treatment on prisoners. An act of abuse did not meet the definition of torture unless the interrogator inflicted pain "equivalent in intensity to the pain accompanying serious physical injury, such as organ failure, impairment of bodily function or even death." In December 2002, Secretary of Defense Donald Rumsfeld agreed to additional interrogation measures, including forcing prisoners to stand for lengthy periods and experience isolation for up to a month. Interrogators could also exploit the phobias of prisoners and use dogs for that purpose (later, after hearing objections from the navy's top lawyer, Rumsfeld rescinded this additional order, pending a study).

Andrew Sullivan, a neoconservative who had supported various aspects of the war, wrote a lengthy review of the evidence of abuse in the *New York Times Book Review*. He concluded, "it seems unmistakable from these documents that decisions made by the president himself and the secretary of defense contributed to the confusion, vagueness and disarray, which, in turn, led directly to abuse and torture." Sullivan maintained that the president "bears sole responsibility" for ignoring Secretary of State Colin Powell's earlier warnings about the vague rules and potential for abuse. Furthermore, "those with real responsibility for the disaster were rewarded" by holding on to their jobs at the beginning of Bush's second term or receiving promotions. Sullivan suggested that Americans who defended the war needed to recognize how important it was to remove this cancer from the system.[16]

Fahrenheit 9/11 did not deal specifically with the abuses at Abu Ghraib and Guantanamo, but it did anticipate the problem of improper dealing with prisoners through its imagery and narration. Moore's film reminded audiences that efforts to deal with the Iraqi insurgency involved the potential for trouble. In many cases, U.S. soldiers had to act as policemen, guards, and interrogators. They received little training for these tasks and lacked familiarity with the language and culture of the Iraqi people. In these circumstances, abuse was likely. The record of harsh treatment of prisoners confirmed Moore's observation that unfortunate consequences can occur when a president makes the mistake of sending good young Americans into a bad situation.

Another important statement in *Fahrenheit 9/11*, regarding the United States' mistakes in Afghanistan, was also supported by later news discoveries. Moore shows President Bush's tough public persona regarding his determination to pursue Osama bin Laden and al Qaeda after the 9/11 tragedy. "We're gonna smoke 'em out," says the president, in the style of a Western movie hero. Yet for all this tough talk, "Bush really didn't do much," says Moore in his narration. *Fahrenheit 9/11* shows Richard Clarke remarking that the Bush administration's response was slow, taking two months for U.S. forces to go into action in Afghanistan, and then with only 11,000 troops. The United States relied largely on anti-Taliban Afghan soldiers of the Northern Alliance to pursue Osama bin Laden, and under those circumstances, it is not surprising that America's nemesis got away.

A story in the *New York Times* in April 2005 appeared to confirm Moore's judgment about the administration's mistakes. The report indicated that "Osama bin Laden had been able to elude capture after the American invasion of Afghanistan by paying bribes to the Afghan militias delegated the task of finding him." A spokeswoman for the head of a German intelligence agency said that Afghan forces told bin Laden that they knew of his whereabouts and that he would soon be arrested; however, they gave the terrorist safe passage in exchange for a bribe. This revelation confirmed not only a problem identified in *Fahrenheit 9/11* but also one specified by Senator John Kerry during his presidential campaign. On several occasions, Kerry charged that the Bush administration had outsourced the search for bin Laden, leaving the task largely to the Afghans rather than the well-trained and strongly motivated U.S. soldiers.[17]

Fahrenheit 9/11 addresses another problem when it shows a CBS reporter referring to the need to find adequate troops to support the occupation. The CBS figure indicates that the Pentagon might have to hold 24,000 combat troops beyond their tour of duty. The film then shows two soldiers talking about the declining number of recruits signing up for the military, the difficulties of retaining soldiers, and their frustration at being deployed for such a lengthy period. By late 2004 and early 2005, this problem had indeed become serious. The head of the Army Reserve warned that his troops were "rapidly degenerating into a broken force." An army personnel officer said, "We're growing increasingly concerned about the health of the force. . . . These deployments are really beginning to take a toll."

Since the army was already stretched thin with commitments in other regions of the world, it had to rely on the National Guard and the Army Reserve. Young Americans evidently began to recognize the risk of signing up for either the regular military or the National Guard, and they worried about the possibility of being sent on a dangerous mission to Iraq. Recruitment for the National Guard soon fell 30 percent below the goal, and the Army Reserve fell short by 10 percent. Desperate for manpower, both groups sweetened the signing bonuses and added more top recruiters. The U.S. military also jacked up its recruitment advertising budget considerably, and it tried to win interest among young people by sponsoring NASCAR racing cars, rodeo riders, football games, and an Internet video game called *America's Army.*

Moore deals with this matter in one of the most memorable portions of his film. He and his camera operators follow two marine recruiters as they attempt to convince young men to enlist at a low-income shopping area in Flint, Michigan. The recruiters sound like used car salesmen as they try to size up potential clients and discuss strategies for approaching young citizens who, in some cases, appear somewhat naive about the encounter. When engaging in conversation with the potential recruits, these marines search for information about the individual's interests and then claim that their organization can provide outstanding opportunities to realize those personal goals. Through these filmed conversations, Moore shows not only why many low-income youngsters view military service as a chance for education and self-improvement but also how the hard-pressed marines and other services are desperate to find additional man- and womanpower.

After *Fahrenheit 9/11* appeared in theaters, some parents became especially cautious about protecting their children from the high-pressure tactics of military recruiters. In the case of an Ohio family, the threat was more irritating than real, because the boy in question was only fifteen years old and a freshman in high school. The young man's stepfather informed a recruiter who called the house that the boy was unqualified because of his age, but the navy made two more calls to the family's home. The boy's mother said, "I saw the movie and thought it was amazing. But now it's happening to my child. Are the armed forces so desperate that they are targeting our kids?" she asked. The mother had a terse message for the navy: "Stay away from my child!" A petty officer and spokesman for the navy's Ohio recruitment office explained that records of the first call to the home had been lost. He admitted that standard operating procedure involved placing ads in newspapers and on the Internet and visiting high schools.[18]

Fahrenheit 9/11's coverage of wounded and recovering veterans at hospitals is emotion laden and sobering. The young men without legs or arms have taken more than just physical hits; they have been wounded emotionally as well. Moore confronts Americans with disturbing pictures that they do not usually encounter when watching the news on television. He also shows several soldiers' coffins draped with American flags, the kind of scene that the Bush administration deliberately tried to keep from public view. These and other images support Moore's argument about the war's impact on young Americans. *Fahrenheit 9/11*'s message is this: These youngsters are paying a heavy price, while many other Americans, especially those far removed from the working classes, view the war from a comfortable distance. They are spared the ugly pictures of wounded and dead soldiers, while poor and lower-class Americans confront these grim realities directly and in increasing numbers.

Finally, *Fahrenheit 9/11* provides an important message about the American people's acquiescence to the president's policies in Iraq. One of the most puzzling aspects of the nation's long and troubled intervention in Iraq was the prevailing silence at home. Compared with Americans of the 1960s, Americans of the 2000s were rather tranquil. There were very few antiwar rallies or peace gatherings in the period before and immediately after the appearance of *Fahrenheit 9/11*. Back in April 1965, however, more than 15,000 gathered to demonstrate in Washington, D.C., just weeks after President Lyndon Johnson committed U.S. troops to combat. Later in the 1960s, hundreds of thousands of protesters gathered to demonstrate around the country. Resistance among Americans in the military was also strikingly different. In the 2000s, only a few veterans and members of the armed services boldly raised objections to the U.S. intervention and occupation, whereas in the 1960s and early 1970s, many soldiers and veterans opposed to the Vietnam War received headline attention for their activities.

Millions of Americans worried about the danger U.S. soldiers faced in Iraq, and they fretted, too, over the possibility that their country might slip into another quagmire like the one forty years earlier in Vietnam. Yet most Americans remained rather supportive of President Bush's efforts in Iraq—certainly more supportive than Americans of the 1960s, many of whom protested loudly against the policies of President Johnson. Why the relative calm?

The answers to such a question are multitudinous and complex, but *Fahrenheit 9/11* offers some possible explanations. Moore features a number of diverse comments in his film that provide insight into Americans' faithfulness to the president and his policies. Most of these observations come from the mouths of interviewees rather than from the narrator. Moore lets

Americans themselves communicate the nature of their loyalty. As mentioned previously, pop music artist Britney Spears provides one of those insights when she tells CNN's Tucker Carlson that Americans should trust the president and support him. This clip drew laughs in the theaters, but Spears's perspective was representative of a large segment of public opinion. Many Americans took a similar position at the time. They trusted their president and remained "faithful," the word used by Spears.

Lila Lipscomb, the most important interviewee in Fahrenheit 9/11, also provides some revealing insight into the absence of dissent, despite the nation's many failures in Iraq. Lipscomb admits quite candidly that she knew little about foreign policy and international relations before her son died in Iraq while serving with a Black Hawk helicopter group. Lipscomb reveals that she considered herself a "conservative Democrat," a strongly patriotic citizen, and an enthusiast of young people's participation in the U.S. armed forces. She remained strongly patriotic after her son's death, but the experience led her to learn more and question more. She tells Moore that she always hated war protesters; she confesses that she thought the protesters were dishonoring her son through their supposedly anti-American activities. In time, she says, she came to understand that "they weren't protesting the men and women that were there [in Iraq], they were protesting the concept of war." Lipscomb acknowledges her earlier ignorance about international matters. "Iraq, Baghdad. I didn't know anything of those things," she says. Later Moore follows Lipscomb in Washington, D.C., where she attempts to release her anger toward the president. Suddenly a woman passerby enters the scene as a counterprotester and challenges Lipscomb's demonstration of grief. "This is all staged," she says. "This is all staged." Lipscomb insists that her son really did die in Iraq and that her grief is sincere. In evident anger, the woman mentions that other young men were killed too, and al Qaeda should be blamed, not the U.S. government.

When Moore asks what all the commotion was about, Lipscomb describes the encounter and offers a penetrating insight. She characterizes the woman's response as ignorance. "Everyday people" think they know what the war is about, Lipscomb observes, but they are badly informed. "People think they know, but you don't know. I thought I knew, but I didn't know." In that brief, perceptive observation, the grieving mother of a dead soldier acknowledges that she and millions of other Americans had little appreciation of the real nature of the war in Iraq when they applauded their nation's intervention and looked critically on those who questioned it. Of course, *Fahrenheit 9/11* aimed to assist that educational awakening by delivering an interpretation that contrasted dramatically with the reports typically broadcast on American television.

Fahrenheit 9/11 was an extraordinarily effective film, although not perfect. Michael Moore could have been more cautious about making provocative and sweeping statements on controversial political issues, and he would have been on safer ground if he had not tried to address so many complex and unanswerable questions in the first hour of the movie. All in all, though, his film represents an impressive example of the power of an entertaining documentary to raise significant questions about public policy and to provoke thought and debate. An overview of the numerous disputes about *Fahrenheit 9/11*'s specific treatment of facts and issues suggests that the film offered a better interpretation of recent U.S. history than many Americans believed during the heated debates and intense attacks on Moore in the national media. Information coming to light after the summer of 2004 appeared to indicate that quite a few of the complaints registered in *Fahrenheit 9/11* were valid. In this respect, Moore was rather prescient about the problematic course of U.S. foreign policy in the Middle East.

But could a partisan film like *Fahrenheit 9/11* affect attitudes and behavior? Might it influence the results of a national election? Did this cinematic provocation advance the causes Michael Moore championed, or did it, ironically, set them back?

6 The Impact of Film

Michael Moore never concealed his goal of making an impact on the 2004 presidential election when he made *Fahrenheit 9/11*. The filmmaker stated frankly that he hoped the movie would help drive George W. Bush out of the White House. Moore did not depend only on screenings of the documentary to accomplish this goal. Through numerous appearances on television programs and through Internet streaming, he tried to draw attention to the issues raised in *Fahrenheit 9/11*. Moore also traveled around the country in the months prior to the election, trying to arouse uncommitted voters to support his perspective on the president and his policies. He focused particularly on young Americans in the eighteen to early-twenties age range—individuals who tended not to take an interest in politics or to vote. If many of them could be mobilized, he judged, their ballots would likely put John Kerry over the top.

Did *Fahrenheit 9/11* have an impact on the 2004 election? What was its influence on Democrats, Republicans, and undecided voters? Can any form of politicized entertainment, whether in the form of a documentary film or a dramatic feature, affect elections or the public's attitude about politics? What kind of evidence supports or undermines the case for claiming a film's influence? For that matter, is George W. Bush's victory in 2004 sufficient evidence to conclude that *Fahrenheit 9/11* failed to wield the political clout Michael Moore hoped it would?

When the election produced a fairly impressive Bush victory, giving the incumbent president a substantially greater lift in popular votes than he had received in 2000, many of Moore's critics concluded that *Fahrenheit 9/11* had failed to make a significant impression on American voters. The movie had played to a hard-core Democratic base, they argued, and Moore had preached to partisans who were already convinced of his cause. Those fans of the film were, for the most part, a fiercely antiwar and anti-Bush crowd.[1] Critics said that *Fahrenheit 9/11* may have excited a few Bush-haters to come to the polls, but it must have aroused pro-Bush Americans to vote as well. The result was probably a wash. The film did not provide the boost to Kerry that Democrats had wanted because it was much too opinionated and unbalanced for the American public's tastes.

General election results cannot bring debates about *Fahrenheit 9/11*'s influence to a close, however. The record of the millions of votes cast for Bush and Kerry does not provide specific evidence of Moore's impact. Perhaps Kerry would have lost by a *larger* margin if *Fahrenheit 9/11* had not been playing in theaters across the country during the summer of 2004 and available for rental and purchase on videotape and DVD in October of that year.

This analysis cannot produce a firm conclusion regarding the film's impact, but the question of its influence is more intriguing and complex than many commentators have suggested. To probe the issue of effect, it is useful to consider some general evidence regarding the influence of popular film on attitudes and the way specific individuals and groups reacted to *Fahrenheit 9/11*. This evidence suggests that movies with emotional clout have the *potential* to shape opinions and stir the actions of audiences. Some films are both entertaining and provocative, and some viewers do not disregard the movies' messages after leaving the theaters or turning off their television sets. They may be swayed emotionally and even politically by what they see on the screen. *New York Times* movie reviewer A. O. Scott contemplated this impact when he observed the excitement over *Fahrenheit 9/11* and other politically oriented documentaries in 2004. Scott said that the popularity of those productions led amazed and bemused film critics "to witness the affirmation of something they often say and rarely believe: that movies have the power to influence political debate, to engage issues of paramount public importance and even to influence the course of events."[1]

Jane Gaines reminds us that addressing the issue of impact is like raising "an almost unanswerable question," because it is so difficult to measure the influence of a film. What are the signs of political consciousness-raising, she asks? How can we measure it? What constitutes "action" in response to a movie's appeal? The idea that films can produce sweeping social change may be a "myth," she suggests, because enthusiasts of committed documentaries often have difficulty identifying specific productions that truly contribute to notable social change. Although the obstacles to proving impact are great, Gaines nevertheless finds evidence of the power of "radical" films to affect emotions. It is at the visceral level (rather than the abstract, intellectual one) that these productions sometimes appear to be successful in influencing viewers. Documentaries may shake the attitudes of audiences when they appeal to the senses as well as to the intellect. A film that achieves some of the purposes of its committed creators can demonstrate the "power of sympathetic magic," making viewers feel concern for the victims of injustice. A documentary's images of violence committed against oppressed minorities, for example, may excite the viewers' sense of outrage and anger. Gaines raises important questions about the ways individuals often react emotionally—almost without thinking—to the shocking evidence they see in the productions of politically committed filmmakers.[3]

A consideration of the impact of committed efforts to persuade through use of the mass media need not be limited to interpretations presented on the screen. Before film there was, of course, the pamphlet and the book, and historians have long recognized the influence of the printed page on the minds of readers. Bernard Bailyn, a noted scholar of the American Revolution, has pointed to the tremendous influence of political pamphlets on the thinking of the colonists, who moved rather rapidly in the 1760s and 1770s from loyalty to rebellion when dealing with their mother country. Thomas Paine's *Common Sense* (1776) argued that Americans had good cause to free themselves from English oppression, and his writing influenced many colonials to make the break for independence. More than a century later, Ida Tarbell's reporting on abuses practiced by John D. Rockefeller and his Standard Oil Company helped open investigations, and actions in the courts eventually led to Standard Oil's breakup under the nation's antitrust laws. In the early 1960s, Betty Friedan's *The Feminine Mystique* helped awaken the women's revolution, and Rachel Carson's *Silent Spring* served as an important impetus for the environmental movement that grew in prominence later in the decade. Historians treat emotion-packed, politically oriented novels, too, as potentially significant influences on national opinion. They note that Harriet Beecher Stowe's *Uncle Tom's Cabin* (1852) excited antislavery feeling. When President Lincoln met Stowe during the Civil War, he said, "So you're the little woman who wrote the book that made this great war." Lincoln exaggerated Stowe's influence, of course, but his observation communicated a sense of the importance of abolitionist literature in stirring public sympathy for the slaves. Historians also point out that, during the Progressive Era, Upton Sinclair's *The Jungle* aroused public concern about the sale of unsanitary food products and provoked President Theodore Roosevelt to demand stronger federal regulatory measures regarding the inspection of beef.

When considering the impact of politically oriented film, many Americans are unwilling to take the next logical step. They are reluctant to treat the moving image on the screen as an extension of the media provocations realized earlier through the printed page. When commentators look dubiously on claims about the influence of film, they manifest an old-fashioned attitude. Like members of the 1915 U.S. Supreme Court, in the decision known as *Mutual Film Corp. v. Industrial Commission*, they interpret books as promoters of ideas but consider movies to be just entertainment. In 1915 the Supreme Court held that the exhibition of motion pictures "is a business, pure and simple, originated and conducted for profit." This definition did not provide motion pictures with the same First Amendment protection enjoyed by the press. The Supreme Court eventually overturned this narrow judgment in the *Miracle* case of 1952. Justice Tom Campbell Clark, articulating the Court's majority opinion, wrote, "It cannot be doubted that motion pictures are a significant medium for the communication of ideas." He noted that cinema "may affect public attitudes and behavior in a variety of ways, ranging from direct espousal of a political or social doctrine to the subtle shaping of thought which characterizes all artistic expression."[4]

Historians and the public would be better informed if they kept this Court decision in mind when approaching the question of the impact of film. A modern view of motion picture and television entertainment suggests that these media may educate as well as entertain, persuade as well as amuse. Cinema, too, can shake up opinions and sometimes change them. Surely some films influence ideas more than others, and *Fahrenheit 9/11* scores very high in any measure of the potential for political arousal, positive or negative.

Is there evidence that some motion pictures *have* made an impact on audiences? The sources for such a consideration are, necessarily, circumstantial, incomplete, and anecdotal. We can never be sure of the number of people affected or the degree to which they were influenced. Nevertheless, fragmentary information hints of the potential of films with provocative social and political themes to move their audiences.

When historians and media scholars consider this question, some of the "films" they study are not feature productions but relatively short pieces that served as newsreels or televised news reports. One of the most familiar cases having to do with an election involved Upton Sinclair's campaign for the office of governor of California in 1934. Sinclair, a socialist, aimed to make EPIC (End Poverty in California) a centerpiece of his campaign. In those hard times of the Great Depression, Sinclair's candidacy looked viable, particularly to Hollywood moguls, who feared that he would appeal to many frustrated, economically deprived citizens. Louis B. Mayer, head of MGM, led the response of Hollywood executives. Mayer threatened to take MGM out of California and bring other studios with him. He appointed Irving Thalberg to create newsreels for screening in California movie theaters that included fake surveys of public opinion. One such interview in a bogus newsreel showed a nice elderly woman saying that she would vote for the Republican candidate because she wanted "to have a little home." In another mock interview, a Russian immigrant was played by a sinister-looking actor with whiskers. When asked who he was voting for, the foreign character replied, "Vy, I am foting for Seenclair" because "his system worked vell in Russia, vy can't it work here?" This brief "newsreel" footage helped discredit Sinclair in the eyes of voters and sink his fortunes in the campaign.

Evidence of the power of brief film and video clips in political campaigns is abundant in the history of modern American presidential elections. In the 1960 contest, for instance, Richard Nixon appeared to be the favorite until he faced John F. Kennedy in the televised debates. The incumbent vice president looked pale and sweaty on television, whereas Kennedy sported a Florida tan, wore makeup, and sounded like he was in command. The debate gave Kennedy valuable momentum.

Mini-documentaries in the form of political ads have served the Republican Party well over the past fifty years. During the 1968 presidential campaign, Nixon's managers succeeded in remaking the image of their candidate through the magic of television advertising. Even though Nixon had lost the presidential contest in 1960 and a gubernatorial race in California a short time later, his supporters used the techniques of Madison Avenue to make him look like a winner in 1968. Their ads showed a warm and caring leader who listened carefully to the concerns of the American people. Promoters "sold" Nixon to the public as they might sell breakfast cereal or bathroom soap, as Joe McGinniss later reported in his revealing book The Selling of the President (1969).

In more recent years, too, Republicans have gained voter support from short and provocative video clips. In 1988 they helped chisel away at Democrat Michael Dukakis's impressive lead in the public opinion polls by featuring mini-documentaries that provided sharply negative pictures of the candidate's leadership in the Massachusetts governor's office. One ad showed pollution pouring into the water of Boston harbor. Another, which became known as the Willie Horton commercial, was one of the most successful efforts in the annals of political advertising. It reported on a Massachusetts prisoner who had won release through the governor's furlough program. Horton, a black man and a convicted murderer, then brutally killed a white woman and terrorized her husband. The ad made Dukakis appear to be soft on crime during a time when the high rates of violent crime troubled many American voters. Mini-documentary ads evidently made an impact in the 2004 election as well. After the Democrats held a celebratory convention that honored John Kerry's military service during the Vietnam War, the so-called Swift Boat Veterans for Truth presented television ads that communicated a very different story. With financial support from anti-Kerry groups, the spots focused on the Democratic candidate's antiwar activities in the early 1970s and suggested that his actions had dishonored fellow veterans. Many political analysts believed that these commercials were critical in weakening Kerry's appeal with the voters.

Peter Davis was one of the most important left-leaning creators of politically significant documentaries in the early years of television. He is remembered especially for his work on groundbreaking films that appeared on CBS Reports; at the time, CBS had the strongest reputation for sophisticated informational programming on network television. Davis helped make *Hunger in America*, which aroused concern about the plight of the poor and provided the impetus for governmental reforms that introduced food stamps. In the early 1970s Davis produced *The Selling of the Pentagon*, which revealed that the Defense Department had been tremendously active at public venues, trying to advertise its importance and win public support for military engagement in Vietnam. Davis's film provoked tremendous criticism because it suggested that the U.S. government had been manufacturing propaganda. Some defenders of the government demanded an investigation of both CBS and Davis. A few years later, Davis released *Hearts and Minds* in theaters, the most powerful and influential of all the early documentaries about the Vietnam War and winner of the Academy Award for best documentary. In this case, Davis's film had a negligible impact, since it appeared as the United States was ending its active involvement in Vietnam, and the American people had lost interest in the war. His film confirmed rather than aroused the audience's sense of frustration, anger, and disillusionment.

Sometimes dramatic films from Hollywood arouse a good deal of political interest and may also affect behavior. A notable early example of interest to film historians is *Birth of a Nation*, the 1915 silent epic from D. W. Griffith.

That popular movie, which focused on conditions in the South shortly after the Civil War, portrayed black southerners and white northerners negatively and presented a positive picture of activities by the Ku Klux Klan. African Americans and liberals criticized the movie for promoting racism. When a group of white Georgians heard that this motion picture was going to appear in Atlanta, they gathered outside the city and attempted to create a new Ku Klux Klan (the organization had been fairly inactive since the 1870s). This marked the beginning of the KKK's revival, and by the 1920s, it had a membership in the millions that included many white northerners and westerners as well as southerners.[5]

If movies can arouse prejudice, presumably they can contribute to the diminution of bigotry as well. Two docudramas about the Holocaust are notable in this regard, because they provoked considerable public discussion about the evils of hatred toward racial and ethnic groups. NBC Television's Holocaust, broadcast in the United States in 1978, excited a good deal of interest in the Jewish tragedy of the 1930s and 1940s, but the film's impact proved even greater when it appeared in Europe. Holocaust drew huge audiences in several countries, and its airing on German television became the subject of a lively controversy. Some authorities working with West Germany's national TV organization did not want to broadcast the movie, claiming that it represented a cheap example of superficial, Hollywood-style soap opera. Thus, Holocaust was aired through local television facilities rather than the national network, and it engendered tremendous audience interest in the country. Thousands of citizens demanded that their schools and their national media discuss the German people's responsibility for the tragedy more openly and honestly. At the same time, legislators in the Bundestag voted to extend the statute of limitations on Nazi war crimes, and many Germans attributed that decision to public reaction to the TV drama.[6]

By the 1990s, when Schindler's List made its debut in Germany, attitudes about the history of the Holocaust had changed significantly. Many Germans welcomed director Steven Spielberg to their nation as an accomplished artist, and they applauded his movie as an important moral statement. A small but significant example of the film's emotional impact was suggested by the actions of a guard at a Swiss bank. He reported to his government that hundreds of documents containing information about the accounts of Holocaust victims were about to be destroyed. When asked why he had blown the whistle on the bank, the guard said that he had seen visions of the Holocaust victims and knew what he had to do because "I remembered the movie *Schindler's List*."[7]

Film scholars sometimes point to *All the President's Men* (1976) as a film that had a specific impact on a national election. Alan Pakula's movie, starring Robert Redford and Dustin Hoffman as investigative reporters at the *Washington Post*, reminded audiences of the Republicans' involvement in the Watergate scandal just a few years before. This was problematic for Gerald Ford, the Republican presidential candidate. Richard Nixon had appointed Ford vice president, and when Ford became president after Nixon's resignation, he pardoned the former president. This decision gave many Americans the impression that the two leaders had been involved in a corrupt bargain. Eventually Ford lost the election to Jimmy Carter by a very close margin. Not surprisingly, some observers wondered if the election results would have been different if negative publicity about Watergate had not been introduced by a Hollywood movie early in the campaign.

Could Michael Moore's *Fahrenheit 9/11* affect public attitudes and the behavior of the electorate? That was certainly one goal of the movie's creator and director when he promoted his film during the summer of 2004. Moore clearly stated that he wanted to arouse the public and stir people into action.[8] Since pollsters continued to report that the Bush-Kerry contest was close throughout the summer and fall of 2004, Moore hoped that his film could help propel Kerry into a distinct lead. If Moore could affect just 1 or 2 percent of the vote, he might produce enough momentum for the Democratic candidate to obtain a victory. One way to accomplish that task was to motivate people to go to the polls, especially those who would not ordinarily turn up at the voting booths. "There's millions of you on the sidelines, and I'm the coach saying, 'Come on, bench, get in the game!'" said Moore.[9] He believed in the power of his movie to turn opinions, and he talked about that potential in an upbeat fashion with the news media. "I believe the film is going to bring hundreds of thousands of people to the polls who otherwise were not going to vote," he claimed. "I think it's going to have a tremendous impact that way."[10] With the election fully in mind, Moore pushed for the release of *Fahrenheit 9/11* in theaters at the end of June and the release of the DVD and video in October 2004. This schedule could, he thought, make the film both profitable and consequential in the election.

Moore certainly aroused the interest of the Democratic Party leadership when his film premiered in Washington, D.C. A vote on a defense appropriations bill in the Senate had to be delayed because so many Democrats had left the chamber to attend the premiere. Barbara Boxer and Tom Daschle were present in the theater, as well as other senators. Terry McAuliffe, the party's national chairman, went to the opening in Washington, as did prominent congressmen such as Henry Waxman and Charles Rangel. Richard Ben-Veniste, who played a key role on the 9/11 Commission, also attended. Some prominent figures from the Kennedy administration appeared as well, including Arthur Schlesinger Jr. and Ted Sorenson.[11] At the end of the screening, hundreds in the audience gave the movie a standing ovation.

Audience demonstrations of appreciation had begun with *Fahrenheit 9/11*'s early screening at the Cannes Film Festival in France, where the movie received a standing ovation. Then the spontaneous applause heard at the Washington premiere was repeated in numerous venues throughout the United States and abroad. "This was a brand new movie-going experience," wrote Denis Hamill for the *New York Daily News*. He had watched the film in a Queens theater and noticed that a rustle of tissues could be heard as men and women, young and old, wiped their eyes as they listened to Lila Lipscomb describe the pain she felt after losing her son in Iraq. Hamill noted that it was unusual for an audience to become so involved in a nonfiction film. This was not Hollywood drama, he emphasized. As at many other venues, there was a burst of applause at the movie's conclusion. *Fahrenheit 9/11* showed real fireballs, real soldiers, and real deaths, Hamill wrote, "and the reason the people in the audience, the American people, get so involved in this movie is because we are all extras in the story." Hamill mentioned with amusement that in Brooklyn, an unemployed construction worker bought a bootleg copy of *Fahrenheit 9/11* that someone had shot in a theater with a camcorder. The construction worker reported that the audience applauded at the end in the bootleg copy as well.[12]

Tom Feran reported a similar phenomenon for the *Cleveland Plain Dealer*. In an article called "Unusual Noise Follows '9/11': The Sound of Fans Clapping," Feran observed that applause at the end of a screening was unusual, because the artist responsible for the production could not hear the demonstration of appreciation. Perhaps, he guessed, the applause represented a form of release for the audience. Feran had heard one moviegoer, a graduate student, express this sentiment. "I felt a sense of relief, with all the anxiety about what's going to happen, that somebody's doing something on a level that grand and broad-ranging," said the student. Feran noted that the appreciative audience he encountered clapped for more than thirty seconds.[13]

When reporting on these enthusiastic receptions, both Feran and Hamill maintained that Fahrenheit 9/11 offered more than just emotional satisfaction to its viewers. They believed that the movie made a significant contribution to the audiences' thinking. Some observers compared Michael Moore with Oliver Stone, Feran noted, but Moore's film did not involve wild conspiracy theories in the manner of Stone's JFK. "You can question the way [Moore] connects the dots," said Feran, "but the dots look more solid than the intelligence that led to the war."[14] Hamill compared the movie to Thomas Paine's provocative pamphlet of the American Revolution, Common Sense. He noted that in Paine's day, Common Sense provided an important new style of political communication about the behavior of leaders in government. If Paine were around today, Hamill speculated, the revolutionary writer would probably try to deliver his message in the provocative, modern form exemplified by Michael Moore.[15] Whereas Paine had called for independence from England, Moore called for independence from the mistaken policies of the Bush administration and independence from the supportive reporting on the war in Iraq by many in the national news media. Moore had been "picked apart by the press" because he challenged the media's presentation of the war, Hamill observed. Journalists, swept up by the post-9/11 patriotic "hysteria," had been compromised when they served as embedded reporters in Iraq. The Bush administration "spoon-fed" jingoistic war news to the journalists, argued Hamill. Moore raised important questions about U.S. actions in Iraq that many media professionals failed to raise.[16]

Small pieces of evidence coming in from newspapers around the country suggested that Fahrenheit 9/11 aroused political interest when it first appeared in local theaters. The Atlanta Journal-Constitution reported in a headline, "'Fahrenheit 9/11' Charges Up Political Talk at Work." The article indicated that the movie was provoking lively discussions around the water cooler, some of which were quite animated and intense.[17] Fahrenheit 9/11 attracted the interest of U.S. servicemen and servicewomen at military bases as well. The Wall Street Journal indicated that soldiers and their families associated with Fort Bragg, near Fayetteville, North Carolina, represented about half the audience in the local Fahrenheit 9/11 screenings. Marines from Camp Lejeune were present too, driving two hours to view the film in Fayetteville. A twenty-six-year-old army machine gunner told the Wall Street Journal's interviewer that he had enlisted the previous year to serve his country and expected to be sent to Iraq. Nevertheless, he found the messages in Moore's movie worthy of consideration. "That's pretty thought-provoking," he concluded. "I guess I'm a little disillusioned. I've got more questions than answers now," he confessed.[18]

Could *Fahrenheit 9/11* inspire Republicans and supporters of President George W. Bush to applaud the movie too? Might it convince some Republicans to choose the Democratic candidate? Republican pollster Frank Luntz conducted a survey in August 2004, just a few months before the presidential election. He found that 37 percent of the Republicans who saw *Fahrenheit 9/11* were much less likely to vote for Bush.[19] This alarming evidence probably alerted Republican leaders to the movie's potential to do serious damage to their party's cause. Of course, if Republicans never went to see the film in the first place, the matter of its influence would prove less troublesome. That is exactly what happened; critics' efforts to discredit the movie as radical, unfair, and an insult to the president led many Republicans to forgo a screening. Carol Bernhard communicated this viewpoint emphatically when she demonstrated against a special showing of the film in Crawford, Texas, near President Bush's ranch. Bernhard and a few friends held up a sign that read, "This is Bush Country." Bernhard declared, "I'm not going to give that traitor any of my money."[20]

The negative publicity given to *Fahrenheit 9/11* by various Bush supporters and some critics in the national media left many Americans with an impression similar to Bernhard's. They did not intend to help Michael Moore become rich. Furthermore, the highly partisan nature of the controversy over *Fahrenheit 9/11* made some citizens uncomfortable about attending a screening where many anti-Bush Americans would be present. They did not want their friends and neighbors to think that they had switched sides and were showing support of Moore's critique of the president. Their presence among the demonstrably pro-Moore crowds at a local theater might leave the wrong impression.

Supporters of the president and critics of Moore sometimes displayed their contempt for the film spontaneously, as did a crowd at the Aladdin, a Las Vegas hotel-casino. During a performance there, singer Linda Ronstadt called Michael Moore a "great American patriot" and expressed relief that "someone is spreading the truth." Ronstadt urged her audience to see the movie. Angry patrons showed their outrage at her comments by booing the performer, tearing down concert posters, and throwing cocktails into the air. About 4,500 people quickly left the theater. The president of the Aladdin, Bill Timmins, told the Associated Press, "It was a very ugly scene—she praised him and all of a sudden all bedlam broke loose." Timmins would not allow Ronstadt back into her luxury suite at the hotel, and he made arrangements for the singer to be escorted off the property. Ronstadt's behavior "spoiled a wonderful evening for our guests and we had to do something about it," Timmins explained.[21]

Some conservatives, Republicans, defenders of the president, and foreign policy hawks in positions of power tried to minimize the movie's audience. They attempted to provoke public boycotts of the movie, urged theater owners not to screen the film, and challenged Moore's advertising by citing campaign finance laws. A few conservatives went to the extreme of suing Michael Moore. Their symbolic efforts in court appeared to be intended primarily to throw a temporary roadblock in the path of the movie's progress and to arouse defenders of the president and his policies, since prospects for a successful suit were not strong.

The right-wing organization Move America Forward attempted to convince owners of theater chains not to book the film. A posting on its Web site said, "We have a right to tell movie theaters we object to their promoting a movie that is nothing more than a political campaign commercial which should be shown at the Democratic National Convention or as an al Qaeda training video before it is shown at our local cinema."[22] Move America Forward spokesperson Siobhan Guiney affirmed the ideals of the First Amendment and said that Moore had every right to make his movie. "But we as customers have the same right to say this is not the type of movie we want to see," declared Guiney. At a time when "our soldiers are overseas fighting for our safety, now is not the time to do a military-bashing film," Guiney explained.[23] Move America Forward's efforts against the movie represented a way of "supporting America's war on terrorism." The organization sent out a bulletin to its readers claiming, "Terrorist Group Hezbollah Endorses Michael Moore Film," indicating that the radical organization had offered to help promote Fahrenheit 9/11.[24] Move America Forward also orchestrated a letter-writing campaign to theaters around the country announcing the goals of a boycott.

The comments of some owners and managers of movie theater businesses suggested that their organizations came under heavy pressure from these letter-writing campaigns. A spokesman for AMC Theatres reported that his chain received about 500 to 600 e-mails and telephone calls a day protesting Moore's movie. Marcus Theatres' spokesman reported that his Milwaukee chain received a couple of thousand e-mails a day during the height of the political storm. Ray Price, vice president of Landmark Theatres, said that his business received about 10,000 complaints via e-mail.[25] Howard Kaloogian, a Republican assemblyman from California and a leader of Move America Forward, may have revealed the true reason for the campaign when he said, "We will consider it a success if the people that go to the movie understand that it is a propaganda piece."[26] Kaloogian's statement suggested that phone calls and letters might not close down the screenings, but they could discredit the film. Earlier, Kaloogian had succeeded in a similar campaign aimed at boycotting CBS Television for screening a docudrama called The Reagans. Kaloogian and other conservatives believed that film was harsh and unfair in its portrayal of the former president.

Other critics of Moore's movie tried different harassment strategies. For instance, an anti-Moore Web site encouraged readers to watch pirated copies of Fahrenheit 9/11, evidently to ensure that viewers would not funnel money into the hands of the supposedly sinister Moore.[27] Another Web site encouraged readers to download a petition demanding the revocation of Moore's Academy Award.[28] Some conservatives also urged boycotts of the work of Hollywood actors who had spoken out against U.S. policies in Iraq or against the president. They recommended a boycott of Sean Penn's film Mystic River because the activist-actor had opposed the war with Iraq. Some pursued legal action, as in the case of members of the Michigan Republican Party, who asked prosecutors in four counties to file charges against Moore for violating the campaign laws by attempting to bribe voters. They noted that the filmmaker had been speaking to crowds of college students, joking that he would give them free underwear and ramen noodles if they promised to vote.[29]

Around the same time, David Bossie, head of another right-oriented group called Citizens United, took more serious legal action. He filed a complaint with the Federal Elections Commission regarding advertising for Fahrenheit 9/11 that appeared on television. Bossie asserted that such ads were restricted under the terms of the McCain-Feingold campaign financing regulations, which kicked in thirty days before a primary election and sixty days before a general election. He claimed that the networks could not air commercials that included visual images of any candidate for federal office. Since commercials for Fahrenheit 9/11 contained pictures of George W. Bush, Citizens United interpreted the ads as a form of candidacy promotion (i.e., negative ads opposed to Bush and, by implication, in favor of Kerry). Bossie claimed that these charges were not an attempt to silence critics of the president; they were simply part of an effort to ensure that the law was applied evenhandedly to both sides in the political competition.[30]

The purpose of Bossie's efforts appeared to be harassment rather than a serious challenge of the campaign finance laws. His charges certainly represented a stretch of the law's interpretation, and the Federal Elections Commission quickly dismissed the complaint.[31] Bossie's gambit also drew fire from Moore, who suggested that conservatives and Republicans played unfairly. Moore declared that the difference between his supporters and his critics was that the former respected the freedom of speech, whereas the latter tried to shut him down when they disagreed with his arguments.

Bossie was familiar with the practice of political harassment. In the days of the Clinton presidency, he had been chief investigator for the House Committee on Government Reform and Oversight. In that position, Bossie had led investigations of the Clinton administration's ties to Chinese espionage and claims that Clinton's campaigns had violated the law. Bossie had also served the Senate as an investigator on the special committee looking into the Clintons' activities in the Whitewater land development project. To strengthen his latest campaign against Moore, Bossie offered tough words in a letter that Citizens United sent to broadcasters. The communication said that if ads for the movie came under the rules of the campaign finance act, "they are subject to the Act's ban on corporate and foreign funding, and are subject to public disclosure with the Federal Elections Commission in Washington, D.C."[32]

Some owners of theater chains did not need to read Bossie's suggestive letter to find reasons to keep the movie off their screens. They did not like Moore's message and chose to take a pass on his film. These individuals gave a variety of explanations for their decision. Some expressed concern that the film might cause a riot. A few maintained that such a fiercely anti-military movie did not belong in theaters when the nation was at war. Some charged that *Fahrenheit 9/11* suggested to the enemy that the United States was a divided nation. R. L. Fridley, owner of the Des Moines, Iowa–based Fridley Theaters, said that his company did not "play political propaganda films from either the right or the left." Fridley worried that the movie might incite terrorism. "Our country is in a war against an enemy who would destroy our way of life, our culture and kill our people," he noted. "These barbarians have shown through [the attacks of September 11, 2001] and the recent beheadings that they will stop at nothing. I believe this film emboldens them and divides our culture even more."[33] The president of Illinois-based GKC Theaters, with more than 250 venues, took a related position. Beth Kerasotes acknowledged Moore's freedom to make his own movie but said, "We trust that our customers will recognize and respect our freedom of choice not to play it." Kerasotes reminded the public that the summer of 2004 was "a time of conflict," when "our troops need and deserve our undivided support."[34]

The Bush administration decided to lay low during this controversy. After Dan Bartlett made his initial damning statements, the president's team followed a policy of ignoring the movie. "The eagle doesn't talk to the fly," said Keith Appell, a Republican consultant and a leading business promoter of Mel Gibson's movie The Passion of the Christ.[35]

The campaign against Fahrenheit 9/11 took an interesting twist in Utah, where it involved efforts to prevent Moore from speaking at a college or, at least, to counter his public appearance with the scheduling of a noted speaker from the Right. Shortly before the 2004 election, Moore set up lectures on several campuses as part of his "Slacker Uprising Tour," designed to encourage young Americans to register and vote. Of course, he also wanted them to vote against President Bush. Even before his scheduled appearance in Utah, Moore's tour was the subject of controversy. Republicans had resisted Moore's planned appearance at George Mason University in northern Virginia and succeeded in canceling the visit.[36]

Prior to Moore's visit to Utah Valley State College, officials at the institution received many e-mails expressing outrage. Some communications included threats, indicating that donors would never commit funds to the college again if Moore was allowed to give his presentation on campus. A father of a student at the college offered to provide a $25,000 check if student leaders would cancel Moore's presentation. Another donor who had been giving money to the college for more than two decades stepped out of negotiations to donate a $1.4 million art collection because of the controversy. A petition got under way at the college seeking signatures from 10 percent of the student body as a first step toward vetoing Moore's invitation to speak. That petition also called for the removal of the student government president and vice president because of their decision to invite Moore to the college.[37] Despite this opposition, many wanted to hear what Moore had to say, and ticket sales were brisk. Within five days, all seats had been sold. The college's leadership thus faced a difficult decision.

Administrators at the college did not fold in the crisis. Instead, they tried to find a way to relieve political tensions by offering Moore's critics a public event of their own. They secured the services of Sean Hannity, the noted right-wing radio and television talk-show host. Hannity appeared at the college before a loud and enthusiastic crowd, including many conservatives. He attempted to intimidate any liberals in the audience by asking them to stand up and identify themselves. Just a few had the temerity to do so, and Hannity responded by mocking them with the call, "Here little liberal, liberal, liberal." During the question-and-answer period, Dennis Potter, an assistant professor of philosophy at the college, tried to ask a critical question, but he had difficulty communicating his point over the boos.[38]

The intense and tough conservative resistance to Fahrenheit 9/11 suggested that many on the Right feared its potential impact. Conservatives, Republicans, and defenders of President Bush's policies in Iraq did not dismiss Fahrenheit 9/11 as merely an entertaining and partisan film that would be forgotten soon after it played in the theaters. They attacked the production as if it were a significant factor that could alter the dynamics of an extraordinarily close race for the presidency. Leaders on the Right worked arduously to discredit Moore's film in the public mind, and to a considerable extent, they succeeded. Words such as "manipulation," "distortion," and "lies" made many Americans suspicious of Fahrenheit 9/11. Voters were unwilling to view the motion picture at their local theaters, or if they did attend, the bad press made them unwilling to join some of their neighbors in giving the movie a standing ovation. Many voters who were still unsure what they would do on Election Day 2004 were unlikely to view Fahrenheit 9/11 with an open mind because of the negative publicity.

Americans who were strongly critical of President Bush and his policies found much to excite them when viewing Fahrenheit 9/11. Many of them reported that their experience in the theater was a sort of spiritual "happening." These enthusiasts of Moore and his movie did not view the film in a passive way. They and their friends cheered and laughed through the two hours, and many of them applauded at the conclusion. It was clear that Moore had done more than preach to the converted. He had energized them and given them hope.

Partisans for each side suggested predictable conclusions about the impact of Fahrenheit 9/11. Defenders of the Bush administration's policies tended to dismiss the movie as over-the-top propaganda that probably angered many voters. They claimed that Fahrenheit 9/11 created a backlash that increased voter support for President Bush. John Kerry, they speculated, was probably hurt by the negative reactions to Fahrenheit 9/11. Many

Democrats and liberals applauded the movie and its maker. They believed that the film helped mobilize the Democratic base and encouraged many angry citizens to go to the polls on Election Day. There were other primary causes of Kerry's failure, they argued; it was not the fault of Michael Moore. This appeared to be the majority position, but there were minority opinions too. Some Republicans acknowledged the movie's power to undermine the president's image and were thankful that the film did not reach wider audiences. Some Democrats expressed discomfort with *Fahrenheit 9/11*, worrying out loud that its strident style may have irritated too many voters.

In this regard, the survey conducted by Republican pollster Frank Luntz seems particularly relevant. His data suggested that many Republicans (and, presumably, many uncommitted voters) would have denied the White House to George W. Bush if they had had a chance to watch the film from a neutral position. Most of them never had that chance, however. The uproar of protest against *Fahrenheit 9/11* in the national media, led by Republican activists and prominent journalists (who supposedly commented on the film from positions of objectivity), cast a large shadow over the production. A history of the brouhaha over *Fahrenheit 9/11* reveals that the movie's most obvious weakness was not its interpretive failures but the public's *impression* of its flaws, which achieved broad currency in the summer and fall of 2004.

Conclusion

When Michael Moore brought out *Roger & Me* in 1989, he helped bring documentary filmmaking to a new level of popularity, and his later productions contributed as well to the cinematic form's progress. By 2004, many documentaries were achieving much greater popularity than in previous decades. Yet there was no precedent for the extraordinary reception given to *Fahrenheit 9/11*, which became the first blockbuster "Hollywood" documentary. It garnered over $100 million at the domestic box office in its first screenings and earned millions more in foreign and home video sales in the following months.

Fahrenheit 9/11 provoked heated discussions in a tense election year. Its release turned into a major political event. Critics and supporters of President George W. Bush's policies hailed or hooted the movie. Excited partisans discovered that arguments about *Fahrenheit 9/11* provided a convenient outlet for the release of pent-up emotions. Divisions between liberals and conservatives, Democrats and Republicans, citizens from blue states and red states found expression in the exchanges about Moore's film. *Fahrenheit 9/11* served as an important point of reference in the nation's cultural and political wars.

When Americans argued vociferously about *Fahrenheit 9/11*'s treatment of recent U.S. history, they often talked about the movie's aesthetics, but their disagreements were more fundamentally about Moore's politics. Commentators spoke frequently about his documentary filmmaking techniques, yet their assessments were strongly colored by opinions about foreign affairs and the looming election. Most, but not all, of those who praised Moore's artistic style happened to agree with his criticisms of the Bush administration's war making and occupation in Iraq. Most, but not all, of those who criticized Moore's production also disapproved of his political stands.

Americans who were angry about President Bush's foreign and domestic programs applauded the film enthusiastically. *Fahrenheit 9/11* seemed to express their disgust over the nation's political direction with greater force than any other film or television production. Fans of *Fahrenheit 9/11* believed that the national news media had been comparatively timid in their treatment of the subjects addressed in Moore's movie. They loved Moore's toughness and directness. No other filmmaker or television personality seemed to make the case against the Bush administration with as much chutzpah, panache, or originality. The genius of Moore's production, these fans sensed, was the artist's skill in turning film and video evidence into debating points for a far-reaching political indictment. Pictures, interviews, outtakes, music, and other elements in Fahrenheit 9/11 contributed to an impressive cinematic brief against President Bush and his policies. Fahrenheit 9/11 appeared compelling in large part because Michael Moore was able to fortify his claims with original evidence. The filmmaker screened statements and actions of political leaders in a manner that undermined their reputations and their causes. Moore relied, too, on the comments of ordinary Americans—soldiers and civilians—to make his case against policies of the Bush administration. This clever assembly of diverse cinematic elements seemed likely to draw a large and interested audience when it appeared in U.S. theaters during the summer of 2004, since Moore succeeded in communicating his thesis in highly entertaining ways.

The sum of the film, then, appeared to be greater than its parts. Fahrenheit 9/11 was more than just a collection of specific criticisms about recent foreign and domestic policies. It made a strong emotional impact. Moore's fans thought that the information in Fahrenheit 9/11 added up to a persuasive charge against the nation's political course. The movie's forceful assault on the president and his administration left many critics of the Bush administration feeling that, at last, their intense disagreement with recent political actions had found adequate expression.

The movie's detractors were equally intense in expressing their discontent. Very few critics took a moderate stand in which they identified specific objections to the film but also recognized its significant achievements. There was not much middle ground in the reactions to Fahrenheit 9/11. When commentators complained about the movie, they often used highly damning language. Many critics accused Moore of violating traditional standards of documentary filmmaking, and they berated him for manipulating evidence and drawing misleading and untruthful conclusions. Several protesters expressed profound disappointment in the production, and quite a few took the extreme position of suggesting—or flatly stating—that Moore had lied about recent events.

Above all, critics of Fahrenheit 9/11 articulated an objection to the movie's partisanship. They stressed the need for a fairer, more balanced treatment of political subjects. Many complained about Moore's hostility toward President Bush and other Republicans. The filmmaker's stridency, they argued, pushed the current election campaign in the direction of more polemical confrontations. American politics needed calmer, more rational advocacy, they counseled, not the contemptuous humor spewed in Fahrenheit 9/11.

Moore's film was not truly a "documentary," these critics judged, because the filmmaker personalized his presentation at every turn. Moore put a spin on all the evidence he used in the film, attempting to shape every story into a form of propaganda against the Bush administration. Journalists from the print media complained vigorously about this strategy, noting that documentary films usually aim to deliver objective and educational interpretations of historical evidence. Other journalists, including some associated with television news organizations, applied broadcast standards in their evaluations. They maintained that the networks tried to offer generally nonpartisan, responsible coverage to the American public. Fahrenheit 9/11, by contrast, had the appearance of a strongly leftist version of current events. It resembled Rush Limbaugh's and Ann Coulter's spin, but from the opposite perspective.

Critics of Fahrenheit 9/11 also emphasized the potential damage that Moore's cinema could do to the political fortunes of George W. Bush and other Republicans. Commentators who were enthusiastic supporters of the president's leadership and policies often stressed this theme. They concluded that Moore's arguments were mistaken and misleading, yet they worried that many viewers would not recognize these supposed flaws. Moore, a radical filmmaker, might have a significant impact on the attitudes of undecided voters, they speculated. In a close contest for the presidency, Fahrenheit 9/11 could provide a vital advantage to John Kerry, the Democratic contender. A hard-hitting and entertaining movie like Fahrenheit 9/11 seemed to have the potential to shape opinions.

Leaders in the Republican Party were especially sensitive to this prospect. In previous election contests, their strategists had demonstrated that cleverly fashioned media imagery could affect voter actions in significant ways. Presidential elections of the television age had been influenced substantially by smartly designed negative advertising that undermined the candidacy of Democratic contenders, such as the commercials used against

Michael Dukakis in 1988. Indeed, Republicans and their supporters gained political leverage against Kerry in 2004 by broadcasting several commercials that made the Democratic contender look like a political flip-flopper and an unpatriotic American because of his antiwar activities back in the days of the Vietnam conflict. Moore's potent cinema, especially its unflattering images of the president in a Florida schoolhouse on 9/11 or looking or sounding goofy before addressing the nation or while speaking to journalists on the golf course, seemed potentially influential as well. The film might achieve notoriety for serving up the most memorable images and messages of the 2004 campaign.

Pro-Bush organizers recognized quickly that they needed to discredit *Fahrenheit 9/11* in the eyes of American voters before the movie began to work electoral magic for the Democrats. In rapid-fire actions that resembled those coming from President Bill Clinton's "War Room" during the 1992 presidential campaign, defenders of George W. Bush attacked Michael Moore's production. They pounded the movie relentlessly in the national media, concealing the political nature of their attacks by focusing on technical issues. Like some of the journalists who objected to *Fahrenheit 9/11*'s artistry, they emphasized aesthetic concerns. Politically motivated opponents of *Fahrenheit 9/11* blasted the filmmaker for abandoning supposedly sacred standards of objectivity in documentary filmmaking. They claimed that Moore had leveled numerous charges against the Bush administration on the basis of weak or erroneous evidence, creating, in all, a film that constituted propaganda, not enlightenment. *Fahrenheit 9/11*, they charged, should be recognized as a disgraceful example of distortion. It was an insult, they declared, to the many artists who cared deeply about designing responsible and sophisticated documentary films.

This effort to discredit the film could not dampen the enthusiasm of many Americans who vigorously applauded *Fahrenheit 9/11*'s interpretation of recent events, but it did undermine the movie's reputation in the eyes of millions of Americans who had not seen Moore's cinema before encountering the well-publicized, blistering reviews. Quite a few Americans who might have watched the movie with an open mind surmised, after seeing the scathing indictments in the media, that the film was an excessively partisan and flawed production, and they chose not to view it at all. Undecided voters—the small but significant portion of the national electorate that Moore desperately wanted to reach—stayed away from the movie in large numbers. In the end, the politically motivated campaigns against *Fahrenheit*

9/11 succeeded to a large degree. Efforts by the detractors helped darken the public reception of Michael Moore's provocative movie.

Critics neutralized *Fahrenheit 9/11*'s significance in the politics of 2004, but questions about the film's significance in history remain open. How should the movie be remembered? To state the fundamental question in simplistic and dramatic terms, did Michael Moore fashion a lamentably partisan and distorted picture of events, as his critics charged, or did he deliver a powerful indictment of recent U.S. policies and actions, as his enthusiasts claimed? Should *Fahrenheit 9/11* be remembered as a disgusting case of cinematic misrepresentation, or should it be cited as an impressive example of documentary film's potential to address important political issues?

This assessment concludes that much of the material featured in the first half of *Fahrenheit 9/11* raised legitimate questions, but Moore's presentation did not have the full effect that he sought. The points raised in this part of the movie had been considered by a variety of serious investigators in books, newspapers, and magazines. Clearly, this information deserved public consideration. Yet much of the evidence presented was complex and multifaceted, and Moore approached far too many subjects in the opening hour. He could not begin to demonstrate that he possessed impressive answers to the many questions he raised. Moore could not adequately report on George W. Bush's past dealings in business and politics, the involvement of powerful corporate and Saudi interest groups in U.S. affairs, the Saudi nationals who left the United States shortly after 9/11, the shortcomings of the Patriot Act, or several other matters that were briefly addressed in the film. The evidence Moore presented to support most of his accusations was intriguing, but it was insufficient to deliver a compelling argument in cinematic form. Critics could easily point to other evidence supporting different interpretations of these events, and they could claim that Moore's hinting of foul play in numerous instances suggested conspiracy-mindedness. In short, the filmmaker's strategy of presenting a wide-ranging criticism of the president in the first half of the movie made the film marvelously entertaining, but it also left the artist vulnerable to a good deal of carping.

There was, of course, a serious purpose behind the movie's first hour of scattershot assaults on the reputation of President George W. Bush and his administration. Shakespeare's famous observation applies: "If you strike at a king, you must kill him." Moore appeared to recognize the truth of that insight and aimed to raise many troubling questions about the president and his policies before addressing the story of 9/11 and the war in Iraq. Moore knew that his interpretation of that history would excite the wrath of many Americans who, for various reasons, would object to a cinematic indictment of the president, who was generally popular in the summer of 2004. If the filmmaker was going to succeed in stirring doubts about the wisdom of the president's actions, he had to question Bush's basic character. That task called for the incorporation of abundant visual and audio footage that depicted the president as a fumbling, indecisive, sophomoric, and indifferent leader when dealing with the weighty responsibilities of his office. Numerous personal strikes against the president in the movie's first hour served the purpose of undermining the audience's respect for him. Moore hoped that these funny but disturbing images would help prepare viewers mentally to accept his damning assessment of Bush's foreign policy in the film's second hour.

It is easy to chastise Michael Moore for failing to recognize some of the risks inherent in his broad assault on the Bush administration. It now seems evident that this approach left Moore open to savage attacks from his critics. Yet the critics' objections ought to be informed by a recognition of the filmmaker's achievements as well. Moore crammed an extraordinary amount of information in that first hour, and he raised serious questions about the workings of U.S. politics. Also, many of *Fahrenheit 9/11*'s best laughs came in the first half. Ironically, the film would have been stronger if Moore had cut out the first hour, but then the film would have been less enjoyable to watch, less memorable, and less distinctive.

Additionally, it is important to remember that Moore constructed his movie under considerable pressure. He had months, not years, to complete his presentation in time for its appearance during the 2004 presidential campaign. In this context, Moore's accomplishment is indeed impressive. His movie communicated poignant messages, delivering them in clear ways through an imaginative mixture of humorous and serious material. In retrospect, it seems clear that Moore could have delivered a more trenchant argument by deleting some of the material in the first half. During the rush of designing and producing the movie, this opportunity was probably not so evident.

Moore's detractors treated *Fahrenheit 9/11* like an anomaly—a rare, over-the-top, unusually radical work of partisan propaganda that had no place in the nation's supposedly cool, reasoned, and responsible discourse on politics. Yet the movie's primary theses were not much different from the major arguments presented in many notable books released at the time, scholarship that made similar cases against the Bush administration's domestic and foreign policies. Two books published in 2004 are especially noteworthy in this regard. The two distinguished authors—Arthur Schlesinger Jr. and Robert C. Byrd—addressed related subjects in a much more serious manner than *Fahrenheit 9/11* did, but each author drew conclusions that paralleled those presented by Michael Moore in his film. Each author delivered his charges against the Bush administration's policies in formal language that was replete with factual references to U.S. and global history. Yet at the end of their studies, these writers arrived at pretty much the same place that Moore landed in *Fahrenheit 9/11*.

Despite similarities between the purposes and conclusions of the authors and the filmmaker, there is an obvious difference in the nature of their contributions. The two authors could reach only small and well-educated audiences through the traditional medium of the printed word. The filmmaker was capable of delivering his message to the multitudes by packaging it in the form of a highly entertaining movie.

Schlesinger, a prolific historian, and Byrd, the longtime U.S. senator from West Virginia, each had a strong reputation as an accomplished observer of U.S. history. Each had an impressive record of public service. And even though each spoke forcefully and angrily about the Bush administration's response to the 9/11 crisis and its actions in Iraq, neither could be described as radical. Both authors championed American democracy and what might be described as middle-of-the-road politics. On many occasions in the past, each had spoken forcefully in opposition to political and social movements of the Radical Left. Schlesinger and Byrd were moderates in many respects, even though they were strongly opposed to the Bush administration's policies.

Arthur Schlesinger Jr. published *War and the American Presidency* in 2004. He was one of the United States' best-known liberal historians and a longtime political insider in the Democratic Party. During the Kennedy administration, he had served as a White House adviser. Schlesinger had received the Pulitzer Prize in history years before and had published many influential books over more than half a century, including *The Age of Jackson*, *The Vital Center*, *The Coming of the New Deal*, *The Cycles of American History*, *A Thousand Days*, *The Imperial Presidency*, *Robert Kennedy and His Times*, *The Disuniting of America*, and *A Life in the Twentieth Century*.

Schlesinger covered much of the same political territory in *War and the American Presidency* that Moore covered in *Fahrenheit 9/11*. Like Moore,

Schlesinger lambasted the Bush administration for taking the United States into war on the basis of "phony intelligence." He argued that the U.S. government had no compelling evidence of immediate danger related to weapons of mass destruction in Iraq. Administration leaders "cherry picked" evidence to make the case for war, Schlesinger charged. Like Moore, Schlesinger bemoaned the lack of resistance to the Bush administration's extraordinary foreign policy initiatives. He noted that there had been "little effective opposition, or even debate." When the Bush administration reversed honored traditions of multilateral cooperation in international crises and resistance to preemptive military actions, many Americans simply rallied around the flag. After September 11, they accepted most of the measures that President Bush and his advisers sought. Journalists acted "shamefully and incredibly," Schlesinger concluded. The news media treated information released by the White House and the Pentagon respectfully but failed to give much coverage to information from individuals that challenged the administration's case for war.[1]

Like Michael Moore, Schlesinger reviewed the unfortunate consequences of that acquiescence. He noted that the public had allowed the executive branch of the federal government to make war without the necessary checks and balances. The U.S. military held prisoners in legal limbo without access to lawyers or families, Schlesinger pointed out, and the Red Cross reported the inhumane treatment of detainees. Like Moore, Schlesinger attributed the reaction to 9/11 and the war in Iraq to many leaders in the Bush administration, but most of all, he pointed an accusatory finger at the man at the top. There had been no popular clamor for a war with Iraq until President George W. Bush led the nation into it, argued Schlesinger. "It took one man to decide for war, and to promote it, sending thousands of troops there while other nations doubted that a war was justified," he said.[2] Schlesinger was just as acerbic in his treatment of the president and his policies as Moore was, but he communicated this protest in the erudite language of a scholar.

The second author, Senator Robert C. Byrd, had climbed to political fame from humble beginnings. He had worked at many blue-collar jobs and went to night school for a decade to obtain a law degree from American University in Washington, D.C. Byrd had certainly not been a flaming liberal in his younger days, for he had briefly been a member of the Ku Klux Klan and had filibustered against the 1964 Civil Rights Act. Yet he changed his views on racial questions over the years, and he apologized often, saying publicly that he had been wrong. On issues of civil liberties and foreign policy, Byrd gained a reputation as one of the Senate's most learned and progressive-minded spokesmen. Fond of quoting the scriptures, Roman history, and the Constitution in his eloquent Senate addresses, Byrd rose quickly to the top ranks of the Democratic Party leadership. He served many years as majority leader in the Senate and then as minority leader. Like Schlesinger, he was an octogenarian in 2004, the year his book *Losing America* was published.

Byrd, in the manner of Schlesinger and Moore, expressed a strong interest in arousing the American people from their political slumber. In *Losing America* he argued not only that the Bush administration's policies in Iraq were outrageous but also that the acquiescence of the American people and the national media in the face of these policy changes was outrageous. "We were following Bush like lambs to the slaughter," Byrd complained, "barely questioning the administration's claims or the certain consequences of war for our people and for that matter, for the people of Iraq." Extraordinary statements made by the president and key officials in the government went unchallenged, Byrd lamented. "Where was public dissent?" he asked. Why didn't more Americans show an interest in rocking the boat? "Was courage such a rare commodity?"[3]

Over the course of 200-plus pages, Byrd covered much of the same ground in *Losing America* that Moore covered in *Fahrenheit 9/11*. Byrd employed only words to criticize the government's actions, while Moore employed words, pictures, and sounds. Like Moore, the senator argued that leaders in the Bush administration used the tragedy of 9/11 to political advantage. The disaster "provided a way to salvage what was fast becoming . . . a floundering presidency," said Byrd, in language that resembled Moore's narration early in the film. Byrd described many of the same situations that Moore illustrated in *Fahrenheit 9/11*: Colin Powell's hyped-up report to the UN about Iraq's weapons of mass destruction; Richard Clarke's testimony regarding the Bush administration's lack of interest in terrorism before September 11, 2001; the August 6, 2001, briefing presented to the president titled "Bin Laden Determined to Attack Inside the United States"; evidence that private contractors expected to gain large fortunes through activities in Iraq during the occupation; the president's landing on an aircraft carrier with the sign "Mission Accomplished" noticeably in the background; and Halliburton's construction contracts and profit making in Iraq.[4]

Like Moore, Byrd directed attention to the consequences of U.S. military actions in Iraq—both for the American soldiers who served there and for the Iraqi citizens. "War is death," Byrd reminded readers, in language that could have served as a voice-over for the tragic images in *Fahrenheit 9/11*. War means "maimed young men and women, grief-torn families, children without parents, and untold thousands killed by our bombs," he stressed. We must never gloss over these realities, Byrd exclaimed. The senator described injured soldiers at Walter Reed Hospital in the manner of *Fahrenheit 9/11*'s coverage, and he complained, like Moore, that the American public did not typically see pictures of this suffering in the newspapers and on television. Byrd also noted that the United States dropped "bunker-busting behemoth bombs" that killed many innocent civilians in Iraq, yet the Defense Department and military leaders bragged about the supposed "precision" of those strikes. "America was fed an antiseptic war," Byrd observed, "while the world had a better glimpse of the true cost of war."[5]

The modes of presentation in *Fahrenheit 9/11* and *Losing America* were dramatically different, yet the political arguments delivered in these two forms of communication were, in many ways, interchangeable. Moore could have borrowed Byrd's framework and used it as a guide for developing "talking points" for his case against the Bush administration. Byrd could have used evidence from *Fahrenheit 9/11* to prepare a list of principal themes and details that merited discussion in *Losing America*. Each critic of the Bush administration's policies finished in the same general place.

In 2004, *Fahrenheit 9/11* was the most eye-opening and provocative statement among the three commentaries. Michael Moore's film articulated and illustrated just about every significant argument that critics of President Bush's policies wished to communicate about the administration's handling of the 9/11 crisis and the United States' invasion and occupation of Iraq. *Fahrenheit 9/11* did not turn the election against the Republican incumbent, as Moore had hoped, but it helped move several vital issues to the forefront of public consideration. Representatives of the country's news media had offered their rather muted coverage of these topics; Moore addressed them much more directly, provoking needed debates about the issues. In this respect, above all, *Fahrenheit 9/11* will likely emerge as a significant source in American political history, for it demonstrated the potential of a feature-length documentary film to engage the American people in lively discussions about important political matters.

NOTES

Introduction

1. Steve Persall, "Fool or Prophet, Moore Should Be Heard," St. Petersburg (Fla.) Times, March 28, 2003.

2. Editorial, Chicago Sun-Times, March 25, 2003, 27.

3. Kenneth Turan on The News Hour with Jim Lehrer, June 25, 2004.

4. Martin Lewis (U.K. distributor of Atomic Café), letter to the editor, Los Angeles Times, July 4, 2004.

5. Christopher Hitchens quoted in Richard Corliss, "The World According to Michael," Time International (European edition), July 19, 2004, 40.

6. Hanna Rosin and Mike Allen, "'Fahrenheit 9/11' Is a Red-Hot Ticket at the Film's U.S. Premiere, the White House Takes the Heat," Washington Post, June 24, 2004; Corliss, "The World According to Michael," 40.

7. David Germin, "'Fahrenheit 9/11' Sets New Documentary Mark, Topping $100 Million," Associated Press, July 25, 2004.

8. Quoted in Gavin Smith's article in New Statesman, July 19, 2004.

9. "Screening of 'Fahrenheit 9/11' Draws Huge Crowd in Bush's 'Hometown,'" America's Intelligence Wire, July 29, 2004.

10. Ron Weiskind, "Moore a Master of Milking Controversy," Pittsburgh Post-Gazette, June 23, 2004, C-1.

Chapter 1: The Reel Politics of Michael Moore

1. Michele Tauber, "Back for Moore," People, November 18, 2002.

2. Ibid.

3. Joe Pollack, "Michael Moore: He's the 'Me' of Roger & Me," St. Louis Post Dispatch, January 19, 1990; Carley Cohan and Gary Crowdus, "Reflections on Roger & Me, Michael Moore, and His Critics," Cineaste 17, no. 4 (1990); Sheryl James, "A Hometown Film Maker's Drama . . . in Wheel Life," St. Petersburg (Fla.) Times, January 21, 1990; Richard Corliss, "The World According to Michael," Time International (European edition), July 19, 2004.

4. Cohan and Crowdus, "Reflections on Roger & Me"; Kevin Dore, "How the GM Chief Turned Out to Be Villain of the Piece," Financial Times (London), April 18, 1990.

5. Tauber, "Back for Moore."

6. Annette Insdorf, "Documentaries Struggle Out of a Straightjacket," New York Times, May 6, 1990, 13; Dore, "How the GM Chief."

7. "Roger & Me Redux," Fortune, April 7, 1992.

8. Ginia Bellafante, "Pranks and Populism," Time, July 25, 1994.

9. Tauber, "Back for Moore."

10. Cohan and Crowdus, "Reflections on Roger & Me."

11. Ibid.

12. David Bensman, "*Roger & Me*: Narrow, Simplistic, Wrong," *New York Times*, March 2, 1990.

13. Tauber, "Back for Moore."

14. Charles Ealy, "Moore's 'Fahrenheit 9/11' Fires Up Debate on Politics, News Media," *Dallas Morning News*, June 22, 2004.

15. Jefferson Graham, "Moore, Filmmaker for the People," *USA Today*, January 18, 1990.

16. David Com, "Pump Up the Volume," *Nation*, August 6, 1998.

17. Bensman, "*Roger & Me*: Narrow, Simplistic, Wrong."

18. "*Roger & Me* Redux."

19. A. McGregor, "A Comic Looks at the Not-so-Funny," *Herald: Nationwide News Limited*, March 23, 1990.

20. Pollack, "Michael Moore"; Cohan and Crowdus, "Reflections on *Roger & Me*."

21. Kevin Rafferty, interview with author, February 24, 2005.

22. McGregor, "A Comic Looks"; Dore, "How the GM Chief."

23. Dore, "How the GM Chief"; James, "Hometown Film Maker's Drama."

24. John Hartl, "A Humorist's Fine Rage—Moore's Documentary on Flint Breaks Rules, Is Tinged with Tragedy," *Seattle Times*, January 12, 1990.

25. Glenn Collins, "Film Makers Protest to Academy," *New York Times*, February 24, 1990, 13.

26. Pauline Kael, "The Current Cinema," *New Yorker*, January 8, 1991.

27. Cohan and Crowdus, "Reflections on *Roger & Me*."

28. Harlan Jacobson, "Michael & Me," *Film Comment*, November–December 1989.

29. Cohan and Crowdus, "Reflections on *Roger & Me*."

30. Jacobson, "Michael & Me."

31. Kael, "The Current Cinema."

32. Bensman, "*Roger & Me*: Narrow, Simplistic, Wrong."

33. John Harkness, "Roger & Me," *Sight and Sound*, Spring 1990.

34. Ibid.

35. Described in Chester Burger, "What Michael Didn't Say about Roger," *Public Relations Journal*, April 1990.

36. Cohan and Crowdus, "Reflections on *Roger & Me*."

37. Nigel Andrews, "Fun Fiddling with Facts," *Financial Times* (London), April 19, 1990.

38. Cohan and Crowdus, "Reflections on *Roger & Me*."

39. Ibid.

40. Burger, "What Michael Didn't Say about Roger."

41. John Lichfield, "Heck, There Goes the Town: 'Roger & Me' 'Exposes' a Motor Giant that Consigned a City to the Rust Belt," *Independent* (London), May 1, 1990.

42. Burger, "What Michael Didn't Say about Roger."

43. Lichfield, "Heck, There Goes the Town."

44. "Maker of Documentary that Attacks GM Alienates His Allies," *New York Times*, January 18, 1990.

45. Ibid. For examples of the ideological splits that began to occur in reaction to Moore's work, see Bruce Bawer, "Ego Trips," *American Spectator*, March, 29, 1990 (for a view from the Right), and Scott Dickers, "The Progressive Interview with Michael Moore," *Progressive*, June 1996 (for a view from the Left).

46. Richard Corliss, "Blood Bath and Beyond," *Time*, October 7, 2002.

Chapter 2: The Anatomy of *Fahrenheit 9/11*

1. Daniel Fierman, "The Passion of Michael Moore," *Entertainment Weekly*, July 9, 2004.

2. Kenneth Turan, "No Holds Barred: Michael Moore's Partisan Yet Provocative 'Fahrenheit 9/11' Commands Attention," *Los Angeles Times*, June 23, 2004.

3. Charles Ealy, "Moore's 'Fahrenheit 9/11' Fires Up Debate on Politics, News Media" *Dallas Morning News*, June 22, 2004.

4. David Germin, "'Fahrenheit 9/11' Sets New Documentary Mark, Topping $100 Million," Associated Press, July 25, 2004.

5. Frank Rich, "Provocateur or Patriot?" *New York Times*, May 22, 2004.

6. Michael Moore's comments on *Fresh Air with Terry Gross*, October 16, 2004.

Chapter 3: A Sinister Exercise

1. Frank Rich, "Provocateur or Patriot?" *New York Times*, May 22, 2004.

2. *Scarborough Country*, MSNBC, June 25, 2004; Richard Corliss, "The World According to Michael," *Time International* (European edition), July 19, 2004; James Bowman, "The Summer of Their Discontent," *American Spectator*, September 2004, 55.

3. Jonah Goldberg, "It's a Wonderful Lie," *National Review*, July 26, 2004.

4. Bowman, "The Summer of Their Discontent," 55.

5. Quoted in an article by Ron Hutcheson about efforts to boycott *Fahrenheit 9/11*, Knight-Ridder Washington Bureau, Knight-Ridder/Tribune News Service, June 23, 2004.

6. Frank Rich, "Spidey Crushes 'Fahrenheit 9/11' in 2004," *New York Times*, July 11, 2004.

7. David Germain, "'Fahrenheit 9/11' Filmmaker Moore Faces Critical Heat over Methods," America's Intelligence Wire, June 25, 2004.

8. Hutcheson article.

9. Letters to the editor, *Sacramento Bee*, July 4, 2004.

10. Mark Steyn, "Bush-Bashing Tract," *Spectator*, July 10, 2004.

11. Mark Kermode, *Observer*, July 14, 2004, 9.

12. Miriam Rozen, "'Fahrenheit 9/11' Fallout," *Texas Lawyer*, July 23, 2004.

13. Andy Thaxton, "Bush Supporters Should Go See 'Fahrenheit 9/11,'" Texas A & M, University Wire, June 28, 2004.

14. Curtis Luciani, "'Fahrenheit 9/11' Has Little Time for Nuance, Consistency," University of Texas at Austin, America's Intelligence Wire, June 25, 2004.

15. *News Hour with Jim Lehrer*, PBS Television, June 25, 2004.

16. Nick Cohen, "Where Have All the Children of the Left Gone?" *New Statesman*, August 16, 2004.

17. Richard Cohen, "Baloney, Moore or Less," *Washington Post*, July 1, 2004.

18. William Raspberry's column appeared in the *Washington Post* on June 28, 2004.

19. Nicholas Kristof, "Moore's Movie Stoking Anger in Americans: The Push to Sling Mud Is Deeply Dividing Americans," *San Antonio Express News*, July 5, 2004.

20. Philip Gailey, "The Election Is Serious, 'Fahrenheit 9/11' Is Not," *St. Petersburg (Fla.) Times*, July 4, 2004.

21. Philip Gailey, "I Went, I Saw, I Haven't Changed My Mind," *St. Petersburg (Fla.) Times*, July 7, 2004.

22. Charles Williams, letter to the editor, *Minneapolis Star-Tribune*, June 29, 2004, 12A.

23. Andrew Sullivan, "Blinded by the Light: Is Michael Moore Actually Mel Gibson's Alter Ego?" *Time*, July 12, 2004.

24. Cathy Young, "Does a 'Good Cause' Justify Demagoguery of '9/11'?" *Boston Globe*, July 5, 2004, A11.

25. David Denby, "George & Me," *New Yorker*, June 28, 2004.

26. Phil Rosenthal, "Who Would You Believe, Us or Moore?" *Chicago Sun-Times*, July 13, 2004.

27. Ibid.; Moira Macdonald, "Documentaries that Matter: Documentaries Have Changed the Way We Look at the Truth and the World," *Seattle Times*, July 15, 2004.

28. Rosenthal, "Who Would You Believe?"

29. Susan Crabtree, "Republicans Take Right Turn with Documentaries," *Daily Variety*, September 15, 2004.

30. David L. Wolper, "The Documentary: Entertain and Inform, Not Just Inform," in *The Search for Reality: The Art of Documentary Filmmaking*, ed. Michael Tobias (Studio City, Calif.: Michael Wiese Productions, 1998), 285.

31. Located at www.Moorewatch.com.

32. David Brooks, "All Hail Moore," *New York Times*, June 26, 2004.

33. Christopher Hitchens, "Unfairenhit 9/11: The Lies of Michael Moore," *Slate*, June 21, 2004.

34. *Scarborough Country*, MSNBC, June 25, 2004.

35. Sullivan, "Blinded by the Light."

36. "Will 'Fahrenheit 9/11' Impact the Election?" *America's Intelligence Wire*, June 25, 2004.

37. "In Defence of Michael Moore," *Arena Magazine*, August–September 2004.

38. Jason Zengerle, "Crashing the Party—Will Michael Moore Turn on the Democrats?" *New Republic*, July 19, 2004.

39. *Scarborough Country*, MSNBC, June 25, 2004.

40. Luciani, "'Fahrenheit 9/11' Has Little Time for Nuance, Consistency"; Cohen, "Where Have All the Children of the Left Gone?"; *Fresh Air with Terry Gross*, October 18, 2004; Sullivan, "Blinded by the Light."

41. "Will 'Fahrenheit 9/11' Impact the Election?"

42. Luciani, "'Fahrenheit 9/11 Has Little Time for Nuance, Consistency."

43. *Fresh Air with Terry Gross*, October 18, 2004.

44. "Will 'Fahrenheit 9/11' Impact the Election?"

45. Reporter: Matt Lauer, CNBC transcripts, June 25, 2004; *This Week with George Stephanopoulos*, ABC News transcripts, June 20, 2004; Michael Barone, "The Company They Keep," *U.S. News and World Report*, July 12, 2004, 41.

46. "Stretching the Truth? Deconstructing 'Fahrenheit 9/11,'" *Irish Independent*, Europe Intelligence Wire, June 26, 2004.

47. *This Week with George Stephanopoulos*, ABC News transcripts, June 20, 2004.

48. Reporter: Matt Lauer, CNBC transcripts, June 25, 2004.

49. *Scarborough Country*, MSNBC, June 25, 2004.

50. "Will 'Fahrenheit 9/11' Impact Presidential Election?" CNN *Crossfire* television broadcast, June 25, 2004.

51. Lauren Burke, "The Docu-Fantasy of Michael Moore: An Extraordinary Number of Conspiracy Claims," *Rocky Mountain News* (Denver), July 2, 2004.

Chapter 4: The Partisan Documentary

1. Philip Rosen, "Document and Documentary: The Persistence of Historical Concepts," in *Theorizing Documentary*, ed. Michael Renov (New York: Routledge, 1993), 66.

2. Michael Renov in "The Political Documentary in America Today: Commentary by Distributors, Exhibitors, Filmmakers, and Scholars," *Cineaste* 30, no. 3 (Summer 2005): 29.

3. Michael Renov, ed., *Theorizing Documentary* (New York: Routledge, 1993), 24.

4. Bill Nichols, *Representing Reality: Issues and Concepts in Documentary* (Bloomington: Indiana University Press, 1991), x, 111, 125, 135.

5. William Stott, *Documentary Expression and Thirties America* (Chicago: University of Chicago Press, 1986), 19–22.

6. Ibid., 21–23.

7. Erik Barnouw, *Documentary: A History of the Non-Fiction Film*, rev. ed. (New York: Oxford University Press, 1983), 114–117.

8. For information about his work, see Douglas Kellner and Dan Streible, *Emile de Antonio: A Reader* (Minneapolis: University of Minnesota Press, 2000), xii, 2, 11, 16–20.

9. McElwee describes himself as a "nonfiction essay filmmaker" and calls his work "very subjective." See his remarks in Liz Stubbs, *Documentary Filmmakers Speak* (New York: Allworth Press, 2002), 97.

10. Bill Nichols, *Introduction to the Documentary* (Bloomington: Indiana University Press, 2001), 14, 20.

11. Annette Insdorf, "Documentaries Struggle out of a Straightjacket," *New York Times*, May 6, 1990, 13.

12. Pat Aufderheide, "The Changing Documentary Marketplace," *Cineaste*, 30, no. 3 (Summer 2005): 24.

13. Alan Rosenthal, ed., "General Introduction," in *New Challenges to Documentary* (Berkeley: University of California Press, 1988), 7.

14. Rene Rodriguez, "Controversial Moore Documentary Stirring Up Passions for Both Sides," *Miami Herald*, June 24, 2004.

15. See Ron Hutcheson article, Knight-Ridder/Tribune Service, June 23, 2004.

16. Daniel Fierman, "The Passion of Michael Moore," *Entertainment Weekly*, July 9, 2004.

17. Ibid.

18. Charles Ealy, "Moore's 'Fahrenheit 9/11' Fires Up Debate on Politics, News Media," *Dallas Morning News*, June 22, 2004.

19. Fierman, "The Passion of Michael Moore."

Chapter 5: Let the Debate Begin

1. Sharon Waxman, "'Fahrenheit' Shows Approval of Audiences and Distributors," *New York Times*, July 7, 2004.

2. Craig Unger, *House of Bush, House of Saud: The Secret Relationship between the World's Two Most Powerful Dynasties* (New York: Scribner, 2004).

3. Craig Unger, "Saving the Saudis," *Vanity Fair*, October 2003, reproduced in Michael Moore, *The Official Fahrenheit 9/11 Reader* (New York: Simon and Schuster, 2004), 259–279.

4. *9/11 Commission Report: Final Report of the National Commission on Terrorist Attacks upon the United States* (New York: Barnes and Noble Books, 2004), 329–330. The footnote appears on p. 558.

5. Gerald Posner, *Secrets of the Kingdom: The Inside Story of the U.S.-Saudi Connection* (New York: Random House, 2005), 15.

6. Kevin Phillips, *American Dynasty: Aristocracy, Fortune and the Politics of Deceit in the House of Bush* (New York: Viking Press, 2004).

7. Timothy Naftali, *Blind Spot: The Secret History of American Counterterrorism* (New York: Basic Books, 2005), 286–308.

8. Elisabeth Rosenthal, "Study Puts Iraqi Deaths of Civilians at 100,000," *New York Times*, October 29, 2004.

9. Stephen Tanner, *The Wars of the Bushes: The Father and the Son as Military Leaders* (Philadelphia: Casemate, 2004), 240.

10. Dafna Linzer, "No Longer Looking for Iraq's WMDs," *Washington Post National Weekly Edition*, January 17–23, 2005, 16.

11. Walter Pincus and Peter Baker, "Data on Iraqi Arms Flawed, Panel Says," *Washington Post*, April 1, 2005, 1, 6.

12. Moore, *The Official Fahrenheit 9/11 Reader*, 289.

13. Todd S. Purdum, "Flashback to the 60s: A Sinking Sensation of Parallels between Iraq and Vietnam," *New York Times*, January 19, 2005, 12.

14. Seymour Hersh, *Chain of Command: The Road from 9/11 to Abu Ghraib* (New York: HarperCollins, 2004); Mark Danner, *Torture and Truth: America, Abu Ghraib, and the War on Terror* (New York: New York Review of Books, 2004).

15. Michael Duffy, "The Torture Files," *Time*, January 17, 2005, 42–43.

16. Andrew Sullivan, "Atrocities in Plain Sight," *New York Times Book Review*, January 23, 2005, 1, 8–12.

17. Richard Bernstein, "Bin Laden Bribed Afghan Militias for His Freedom, German Says," *New York Times*, April 13, 2005, A12.

18. Sam Fulwood III, "Chagrin Falls: Real-Life Slice of 'Fahrenheit 9/11,'" *Cleveland Plain Dealer*, July 10, 2004.

Chapter 6: The Impact of Film

1. Byron York maintained that the film played well in the blue (Democratic) states but had relatively little impact in the red (Republican) states. See "Campaign 2004—The Passion of Michael Moore—Fun and Games with 'Fahrenheit 9/11,'" *National Review*, April 25, 2005.

2. A. O. Scott, "A New Market for Bravehearts?" *New York Times*, July 11, 2004.

3. Jane Gaines, "Political Mimesis," in *Collecting Visible Evidence*, ed. Jane Gaines and Michael Renov (Minneapolis: University of Minnesota Press, 1999), 84–102.

4. Edward de Grazia and Roger K. Newman, *Banned Films: Movies, Censors and the First Amendment* (New York: R. R. Bowker, 1982), 80–83.

5. Robert Brent Toplin, *Reel History: In Defense of Hollywood* (Lawrence: University Press of Kansas, 2002), 184–188.

6. Ibid., 188–195.

7. Ibid., 196.

8. See Gavin Smith's article in *New Statesman*, July 19, 2004.

9. Richard Corliss, "The World According to Michael: Taking Aim at George W., a Populist Agitator Makes Noise, News, and a New Kind of Political Entertainment," *Time International* (European edition), July 19, 2004, 40.

10. David Germain, "'Fahrenheit 9/11' Sets New Documentary Mark, Topping $100 Million," Associated Press, July 25, 2004.

11. David Brooks, "All Hail Michael Moore," *New York Times*, June 26, 2004, A13.

12. Denis Hamill, "Moore's Message Delivered, Big-Time," *New York Daily News*, June 29, 2004.

13. Tom Feran, "Unusual Noise Follows '9/11': The Sound of Fans Clapping," *Cleveland Plain Dealer*, July 4, 2004.

14. Ibid.

15. Hamill, "Moore's Message Delivered, Big-Time."

16. Ibid.

17. Tammy Joyner, "'Fahrenheit 9/11' Charges Up Political Talk at the Water Cooler," *Atlanta Journal-Constitution*, July 3, 2004.

18. Sharon Waxman, "Urban Movie Goers for Anti-Bush Documentary, Suburban Audiences for Religious Epic," *New York Times*, July 13, 2004; Shailagh Murray, "'Fahrenheit 9/11' Has Recruited Unlikely Audience: U.S. Soldiers," *Wall Street Journal*, July 12, 2004.

19. Judy Bachrach, "The Provocateur: Moore's War," *Vanity Fair*, March 2005.

20. Angela K. Brown, "Screening of 'Fahrenheit 9/11' Draws a Large Crowd in Bush's 'Hometown,'" *America's Intelligence Wire*, July 29, 2004.

21. Adam Goldman, "Las Vegas Casino Boots Singer Linda Ronstadt after She Praises Moore's 'Fahrenheit 9/11,'" *America's Intelligence Wire*, July 20, 2004.

22. Rene Rodriquez, "Controversial Moore Documentary Stirring Up Passions from Both Sides," *Knight-Ridder/Tribune News Service*, June 6, 2004.

23. Duane Dudek, "'Fahrenheit 9/11' Gets Hotter with Controversy," *Milwaukee Journal Sentinel*, June 24, 2004.

24. Gregg Kilday, "'Fahrenheit' Fight Nears Boiling Point This Week," *Hollywood Reporter*, June 18, 2004, 8.

25. Dudek, "'Fahrenheit 9/11' Gets Hotter with Controversy."

26. Sarah G. Berger, "Analysis: 'Fahrenheit 9/11' Effect on Film," *UPI Perspective*, June 21, 2004.

27. "'Fahrenheit' Leak Burns Lion's Gate: Anti-Moore Web Site Urges Users to Watch Pirated Documentary," *Hollywood Reporter*, July 1, 2004.

28. "Why Michael Moore Gets under the Skin of Conservatives," *Salt Lake City Tribune*, October 17, 2004.

29. Ibid.

30. Gabriel Snyder and Susan Crabtree, "Feds May Call for Less of Moore Promos," *Daily Variety*, June 25, 2004.

31. "'Fahrenheit 9/11' Cool," *Hollywood Reporter*, August 6, 2004, 3.

32. David N. Bossie, "Moore for Less," *Washington Times*, November 8, 2004.

33. "Owner of Iowa, Nebraska Theaters Won't Show Documentary 'Fahrenheit 9/11,'" *America's Intelligence Wire*, July 3, 2004.

34. See the article by Anthony Zoubek listed as Illinois State University, "Illinois Kindling Keeps 'Fahrenheit 9/11' Burning," *America's Intelligence Wire*, August 26, 2004.

35. Avery Johnson and Merissa Marr, "'Fahrenheit 9/11' Is Raising Conservatives' Temperature," *Wall Street Journal*, June 30, 2004.

36. Erin Strout, "Planned Visit by Liberal Filmmaker Has Donors Threatening to Cut Off Utah Valley State College," *Chronicle of Higher Education*, October 15, 2004.

37. Laura Werner, "Anti-Moore Petition Is Circulating at UVSC," *Deseret Morning News* (Salt Lake City), September 21, 2004.

38. Ibid.; Strout, "Planned Visit by Liberal Filmmaker."

Conclusion

1. Arthur Schlesinger Jr., *War and the*

American Presidency (New York: W. W. Norton, 2004), III, 28, 38, 40, 29, 33, 23–34.

2. Ibid., 37.

3. Robert C. Byrd, *Losing America: Confronting a Reckless and Arrogant Presidency* (New York: W. W. Norton, 2004), 184, 186, 171, 185, 196; on the media, see 142–143.

4. Ibid., 20, 200, 197, 200.

5. Ibid., 143, 144, 195, 143.

INDEX